Furniture Refinishing
And Repair Made Easy

Contents

Printed and bound by Graficki Zavod Hrvatske & Printing House Founded 1874
2 3 4 5 6 7 8 9 10

Library of Congress Catalog Card Number: 80-81974

Cover Design: Frank E. Peiler
Cover Photography: Dave Jordano Photography Inc.
Illustrations: Clarence A. Moberg
Acknowledgments: The Editors of Consumer Guide® wish to thank the following persons and organizations for furnishing photographs of woods: Larry Frye, Fine Hardwoods Association; Forest Products Laboratory, Forest Service, USDA; and the California Redwood Association. We would also like to thank The Practical Tiger Inc. of Evanston, Illinois, and Wood World of Morton Grove, Illinois, for allowing us to photograph some of their products.

Chapter 1

Style and Substance: How to Recognize Good Furniture

What makes furniture good? All furniture can be evaluated in terms of style and substance, design and construction; but where refinishing is concerned, the criteria for "good" can be narrowed. There is plenty of good new furniture, but for refinishing purposes, unfinished furniture is the real bargain. Then there is good old furniture, which can be divided into four general categories: very old antiques, reproductions, recent antiques, and just plain old furniture. In most cases, only two of these types should be refinished by a nonprofessional—recent antiques and just plain old furniture. Very old antiques and good old reproductions should be restored by a professional; a brand-new refinished look would reduce their value considerably.

Refinishing covers a wide range, from slapping a coat of enamel on a hand-me-down dresser to complete, painstaking restoration. Refinishing and repairing furniture well takes very little skill, but it does take both common sense and a little know-how. Armed with these two basics, you can add value to old furniture, rescue a piece from the junk heap, save a considerable amount of money, and have considerable fun in the process.

Whether a piece of furniture should be refinished depends on several factors. First, what type of furniture is it? Was it good in the first place? If it's an old antique, you shouldn't touch it; if it's real junk, it isn't worth your time. Second, is it something you like and can use? If not, keep looking. Finally, is it well built, and is it in good enough shape to be worth repairing and refinishing? Structural damage is not always repairable; poor workmanship can't always be repaired—and a piece of furniture is worthless if you can't fix it. Before you refinish any piece of furniture, evaluate its style and its substance, and then decide whether it's worth saving.

THE STYLE: WHEN IS OLD AN ANTIQUE?

When you want a piece of furniture to refinish, the best place to look is the family storeroom—the attic, the basement, the garage, or wherever unwanted furniture has collected. You may also discover a real antique or two—pieces handed down through the family for generations. Other good sources are secondhand stores, household auctions, and garage sales; with furniture, as with anything else, one man's junk is another man's treasure.

Antique stores are usually not a good place to look. Reliable dealers do have real antiques, but most furniture there has already been refinished, and you can expect to pay a good price for it. If you're interested in antiques, recent or old, do some research before you buy anything. Real antiques and many reproductions are extremely valuable, but there are also many imitations—if you aren't sure an antique is *really* antique, pay for an expert opinion. Never buy an antique, or try to refinish it, until you know what you have.

There are many different styles of furniture, and each type has distinguishing features. For the most part, the furniture you'll encounter will probably be limited to traditional English and American Colonial styles; you aren't likely to find a Louis XV chair at a garage sale. The basic English and American styles run the gamut from ornate to severely functional, from massive to delicate, as listed in the accompanying table—if you like it, the style is right.

Antiques in the United States are judged in several ways. To some people, an antique is something that's more than 100 years old; to others, any antique worthy of the name was made in the 1700s or earlier. In the East, an antique is Queen Anne or earlier; in the West,

Basic Furniture Styles—English

Style	Period	Woods Used	Description
Queen Anne	Early 18th century	Walnut; also cherry, mahogany, maple, oak	Graceful curves; curved (cabriole) leg, with no rungs or stretchers; minimal decoration, very simple; scallop-shell motif.
Georgian	18th century	Mahogany	
—*Chippendale*	Late 18th century	Mahogany	Elaboration of Queen Anne; ornate carvings, either delicate or bold; many themes, including rococo, English, Chinese, Greek classic; intricate chair backs.
—*Adam*	Late 18th century	Mahogany	Straight, slender lines; heavy Greek classic influence; fluted columns; delicate low-relief carvings, especially draped garlands.
—*Hepplewhite*	Late 18th century	Mahogany; satinwood inlay/ veneer	Based on Adam; straight tapered legs; shield-, oval-, or heart-shaped chair backs; less decoration; delicate carvings.
—*Sheraton*	Late 18th century	Mahogany	Similar to Hepplewhite and other Georgian styles; straighter, more upright lines; Greek classic influence; lyre-shaped chair backs; inlays and thick veneers.
Regency	Early 19th century	Mahogany	Simple, bold curves; smaller scale; more functional, more intimate; colors used.
Victorian	Late 19th century	Mahogany, walnut, rosewood	Heavy, massive, substantial; dark finish; clumsy design; ornate carvings and decorations; marble tops used.

Basic Furniture Styles—American

Style	Period	Woods Used	Description
Early Colonial	17th century	Pine; birch, maple, walnut	Hybrid of English styles; square lines; solid construction; heavy decoration and carving.
Late Colonial	18th century	Pine; mahogany	Imported wood; interpretations of Queen Anne and Georgian styles; formal. Windsor chair.
Federal	Early 19th century	Mahogany, cherry	Interpretations of Georgian styles; Duncan Phyfe variations of Sheraton style; some French influence; heavier versions of English styles. Boston rocker, Hitchcock chair.
Pennsylvania Dutch	Late 17th to mid-19th century	Maple, pine, walnut, fruitwoods	Solid, plain; Germanic style; colorful painted Germanic decorations.
Shaker	Late 18th to mid-19th century	Pine; maple	Severely functional; no decoration; superior craftsmanship; excellent design.

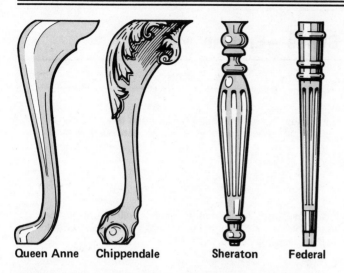

Queen Anne   **Chippendale**   **Sheraton**   **Federal**

Chair and table legs exhibit many of the features that distinguish furniture styles; the leg is usually a good indicator of type. Early Georgian furniture is based on Queen Anne; later styles show classic influence.

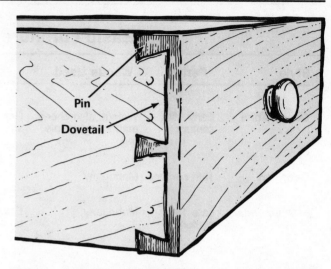

Pin

Dovetail

It's easy to spot an antique by the drawers, because joints weren't machine-cut until about 1860. Look at the dovetail joints; if there are only a few dovetails, with pins narrower than the dovetails, the joint was made by hand.

One of the most popular American pieces is the Windsor chair, designed in the late Colonial period and usually made of pine. Its simple, functional lines, refined still further, are echoed later in Shaker furniture.

it's any piece of furniture that came across the mountains in a wagon. A southern antique is a piece made before the Civil War. Wherever you look, it's a sure bet that you won't find a genuine antique from 1500 or 1600. What you may find is a genuine reproduction, and these can be extremely valuable.

There are several ways you can spot an antique. The first giveaway is the joinery; machine-cut furniture wasn't made until about 1860. If the piece has drawers, remove a drawer and look closely where the front and back of the drawer are fastened to the sides of the drawer. If a joint was dovetailed by hand, it has only a few dovetails, and they aren't exactly even; if it has closely spaced, precisely cut dovetails, it was machine-cut. Handmade dovetails almost always indicate a piece made before 1860. Look carefully at the bottom, sides, and back of the drawer. If the wood shows nicks or cuts, it was probably cut with a plane, a spokeshave, or a drawknife. Straight saw marks also indicate an old piece; if the wood shows circular or arc-shaped marks, it was cut by a circular saw, not in use until about 1860.

Exact symmetry is another sign that the piece was machine-made. On handmade furniture, rungs, slats, spindles, rockers, and other small-diameter components are not uniform. Examine these parts carefully; slight differences in size or shape are not always easy to spot. A real antique is not perfectly cut; a reproduction with the same components is, because it was cut by machine.

The finish on the wood can also date the piece. Until Victorian times, shellac was the only clear surface finish; lacquer and varnish were not developed until the mid-1800s. The finish on a piece made before 1860 is usually shellac; if the piece is very old, it may be oil, wax, or milk paint. Fine old pieces are often French-polished, a variation of the shellac finish. A lacquer or varnish finish is a sure sign of later manufacture.

Testing a finish isn't always possible in a dealer's showroom, but if you can manage it, identify the finish before you buy. Test the piece in an inconspicuous spot with denatured alcohol; if the finish dissolves, it's shellac. If the piece is painted, test it with ammonia; very old pieces may be finished with milk paint, which can be removed only with ammonia. If the piece of furniture is very dirty or encrusted with wax, clean it first with a mixture of denatured alcohol, white vinegar, and kerosene, in equal parts.

The wood itself is the final clue. Very early furniture—before 1700—is mostly oak, but from 1700 on, mahogany and walnut were widely used. In America, pine has always been used because it's easy to find and easy to work; better furniture may be made with maple, oak, walnut, cherry, or mahogany. But because the same woods have always been favored for furniture, workmanship and finish are probably a better indicator of age than the wood itself.

THE SUBSTANCE: FURNITURE WOODS AND WOODWORKING

Almost any type of wood could be used to build furniture, but some woods have always been favored for their beauty, durability, and workability. Before 1900, most furniture was made with these woods; walnut, oak, mahogany, rosewood, fruitwoods, and rare wood veneers and inlays were in common use. American Colonial furniture, dependent on local availability, was made with maple, oak, walnut, birch, and cherry, as well as pine. The preferred furniture woods were readily available, so less attractive or durable woods were used only for hidden parts inside a piece. For this reason, pre-1900 furniture is almost always worth restoring.

As these preferred woods have become scarcer and more expensive, furniture has been made with more abundant woods; the traditional favorites have become rare. Today, most furniture is made with ash, pine, gum, and poplar; pine, fir, and other inexpensive woods are used for hidden parts. The rare woods are used only for very good furniture, and they're often used in combination with the less expensive woods.

Before you can refinish any piece of furniture, you'll have to know what you're dealing with. Woods have different characteristics, and they react differently to finishing techniques; moreover, identification can also help you determine the value of the piece. And wood identification can sometimes be the deciding factor when you aren't sure a piece is worth refinishing. There's a good chance that a beat-up old dresser, for instance, was built with what today is considered a rare wood.

Don't expect to just look at a piece of furniture and know what it's made of—even experts have been fooled by a good disguise. The only sure way to identify the wood is to remove some of the old finish, or to find an unfinished part. You'll probably have a good idea what the wood is before you strip it, but you may get a few surprises once in a while.

Hardness

The simplest way to describe a wood is to say it's a hardwood or a softwood, but this description can be deceptive: not all hardwoods are hard, and not all softwoods are soft. The hard/soft classification is a botanical one—hardwoods are flowering trees; softwoods are conifers. Although most hardwoods are harder than most softwoods, there are exceptions.

In general, hardwoods are more valuable than softwoods, because the wood is scarcer. But this isn't always the case—gum, for instance, is a hardwood that competes in price with softwoods. A more practical way to identify wood is by its grain and color.

Wood Grain and Color

The cell structure of a tree, different for each species, determines its grain. Hardwoods have tubular cells called vessels, visible as pores in the wood. If the cells are large, the texture of the wood is slightly rough, or open; a filler may be needed to smooth the surface. If the cells are small, the texture is smooth; these woods, described as close-grained, don't require filling. Oak, walnut, ash, mahogany, rosewood, and teak are all open-grained woods; beech, birch, maple, cherry, satinwood, gum, and poplar are close-grained. Softwoods don't have vessel cells, but for all practical

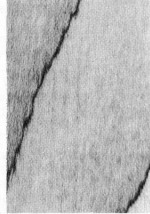

In open-grained woods such as oak and mahogany, there are tubular cells visible on the surface as open pores (left); in close-grained woods such as maple (right), these open pores are not present.

purposes can be considered close-grained.

All trees have annual growth rings, made up of the cells formed during each year's growing season. The types and arrangement of the cells determine how the wood looks. There are woods with subdued and with clearly defined grains; there are straight grains, stripes, swirls, waves or curls, ripples, eyes, and mottled effects. There are colors from white and pale yellow through red, purple, and black. Every species has its own particular grain and color, and although they vary from tree to tree, these characteristics can almost always be used to identify the wood.

Furniture woods are chosen and valued for the character of their grain and color. Hardwoods usually have a richer and finer-textured grain than softwoods, but there are rich grains of all colors and patterns. Woods with very distinctive patterns are usually more valuable than woods with subdued or indistinct patterns, and the weaker-grained woods are often stained to give them character. This is why the old finish must be completely removed before you can tell for sure what wood a piece of furniture is made of.

How to Identify Woods

Once you've removed the old finish, you can make your final identification. This may seem hard at first, but you'll find it easier as you gain experience. With practice, you may be able to recognize various woods by smell and touch as well as by color and grain.

First, consider the piece of furniture itself. About how old is it, and what style is it? Some types of furniture are made with specific woods—ash, for instance, is widely used in bentwoods—and most new furniture is made with woods not used for older furniture.

Second, look at the color. Although color can vary considerably from tree to tree, its tone is fairly constant within a species; the color intensity may change, but not the quality. Some woods have very distinctive color characteristics—poplar, for instance, is the only wood with a green tinge to it, and rosewood can be dark purple.

Finally, look at the grain. Is the wood open- or close-grained? Are the pores evenly distributed, or are they concentrated at the growth rings? Is the grain straight or wavy, mottled or swirled? Compare the wood to the photographs below, and check your guess against the species descriptions.

Veneers and Inlays. Because rare woods are scarce, and because they've always been more expensive than other woods, many types of furniture, both new and old, are made with veneer, a thin layer of wood glued to a base of less expensive wood or plywood. In old furniture, veneers and inlays of rare woods were often used to form designs or special effects; highly figured burl woods and other exotic woods were especially prized. In modern furniture, veneers

are used primarily where solid wood is unavailable or too expensive.

Many different woods are used for veneers and inlays. Some veneers are cut from the crotch or butt of a tree, where the grain is more interesting; some are cut at an angle to produce a particular pattern. Some highly prized grain patterns, such as the bird's-eye figure in maple and the burl patterns, result from irregular growth. Some veneer woods, such as the burl woods, are not usable for solid construction because the wood isn't strong enough. Ebony, in contrast, is veneered because it's much too heavy to be used alone.

Veneers are fragile, and they can be damaged by refinishing techniques; they are the one exception to the identify-after-stripping rule. This means that you should try to spot a veneer before the old finish is removed. Veneers are common in modern furniture construction, so take a good look at your furniture before you start to work on it. Any highly figured wood is probably a veneer.

It isn't always obvious what's veneered and what's not. Sometimes the veneer is visible at the edge of the wood surface, a thin layer glued over the base wood. If you can't see a joint at the edge, look at an unfinished area under the piece of furniture. If the unfinished wood looks the same as the finished surface, the piece of furniture is probably solid wood. If there's a considerable difference, it's probably veneered, and it will require extra care in finishing. Do not bleach, stain, or fill any fine old veneer or inlay.

Combinations. Another consideration is that many types of modern furniture are made with two or more kinds of wood, to keep the cost down. Rare woods are used where appearance is important, such as tabletops; the more common woods are used for less conspicuous structural pieces, such as table and chair legs. This multiple-wood construction isn't always easy to see until the old finish is removed—a table you think is walnut, for example, may turn out to have gum legs, stained to match.

Furniture made with more than one wood needs special refinishing treatment. If you find yourself with a multiple-wood piece, you may have to stain and finish the common wood again to match the wood of the most conspicuous surface.

Common Furniture Woods

Ash (white ash). Ash is a tough hardwood known primarily for its excellent bending abilities; it's used for bentwoods and for bent furniture parts requiring maximum strength. Ash veneers are also common. Ash varies in color from creamy white or gray with a light brown cast to a dark reddish brown. The grain is distinct and quite pleasing when the wood is finished naturally; stains should be used only to change the color of the wood. The wood is open-grained, and can be filled

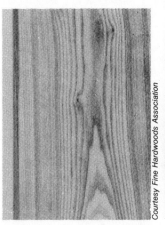

Ash

Basswood

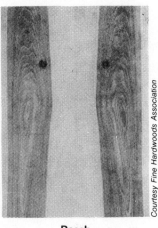

Beech

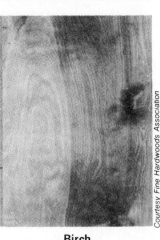

Birch

Courtesy Fine Hardwoods Association

Courtesy Forest Products Laboratory

Courtesy Fine Hardwoods Association

Courtesy Fine Hardwoods Association

or left unfilled. Ash bleaches well, and is easy to work, but it sometimes has a tendency to split. The price is moderate.

Basswood. Basswood is a common hardwood, often used in combination with rare woods such as walnut and mahogany. Its color varies from creamy white to creamy brown or reddish, with broad rays and sometimes slightly darker streaks. The grain is straight and even. Basswood is close-grained, with very small pores; filling is not required. Basswood stains well, and is often stained to resemble cherry, mahogany, and walnut. It is one of the softest hardwoods, and is easy to work with hand tools. It is inexpensive.

Beech. Beech is another hardwood that bends easily, but it isn't as attractive as ash. Beech is often used with more expensive woods, primarily in inconspicuous places—chair and table legs, drawer bottoms, sides and backs of cabinets. Some inexpensive furniture and veneers are made of beech. The color varies from reddish white to reddish brown; the grain is fine-textured, and is identifiable by its conspicuous rays or streaks. Beech is close-grained, and does not require a filler. Staining is not necessary, but beech takes a stain well, and is often stained to look like mahogany, maple, or cherry. Beech is both hard and heavy, and is difficult to work with hand tools. It is inexpensive.

Birch (yellow birch). Birch, a common hardwood, is used in all aspects of furniture construction. The wood is light yellowish brown, very similar in color and in grain to maple. The grain is quite pleasing. Birch is close-grained, so no filler is required. The wood is usually not stained, but it takes a stain well, and is sometimes stained to look like cherry. A clear sealer should be used before finishing. Birch is both hard and heavy, and is difficult to work with hand tools. It is moderately expensive.

Butternut. This hardwood, often called white walnut, is similar in many ways to walnut. The wood is light brown, with occasional dark or reddish streaks; the grain is pronounced and leafy. Butternut is coarse-textured, with visibly open pores; it is usually filled. Butternut stains well, and is often stained to look like dark walnut. The wood is light, and is easy to work with hand tools. It is moderately expensive.

Cedar (Eastern red cedar). Cedar, a softwood, is used primarily in chests and closets; it has a distinctive scent, and is effective in repelling insects. The wood is a light red, with light streaks and knots; the grain is quite pleasing. Cedar is close-grained, and does not require a filler. It should not be bleached or stained. Cedar storage chests should be left unfinished on the inside, and treated with a clear finish on the outside. Cedar is moderately expensive.

Cherry (black cherry). Cherry, one of the most valued of hardwoods, is used in fine furniture and cabinets. Its color varies from light brown to dark reddish brown, and it has a very attractive and distinctive grain, often with a definite mottle. Cherry is close-grained, and does not require a filler. It should not be bleached or stained, although a light stain is sometimes used to accentuate the color. Cherry is difficult to work with hand tools, and it is expensive.

Elm (rock elm, American elm). This hardwood has excellent bending qualities; it's used in all types of furniture, and especially for bentwoods. Elm is light brown to dark brown, often with some red streaks. Elm has a distinct grain; rock elm has contrasting light and dark areas. The wood is open-grained, and is often filled. Staining is not necessary, but elm is often stained to look like walnut or mahogany. American elm is moderately hard; rock elm is hard, and difficult to work with hand tools. Because Dutch elm disease has destroyed

Butternut

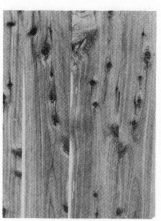

Cedar

Cherry

Elm

so many trees, elm has become a rare wood, and can be both hard to find and expensive.

Gum (sweetgum, red gum). This hardwood is often used in veneers or in combination with rare woods; it's also used in some moderately priced furniture. Gum is an even brown, with a reddish cast; it sometimes has darker streaks. The wood is close-grained, and does not require a filler. Because the grain is usually not strong, gum is usually stained, most often to oak, maple, cherry, or mahogany color. Gum is hard and moderately heavy, and can be difficult to work with hand tools. Its price is moderate to low.

Hickory (shagbark hickory). This hardwood is noted for its strength, hardness, and toughness; it is used in rockers, Windsor chairs, lawn furniture, and some veneers. The wood is brown to reddish brown, with a straight, indistinct grain; it is open-grained, and is usually filled. Hickory is very hard and heavy, and is difficult to work with hand tools. Its price is moderate.

Lauan (red lauan, white lauan). This hardwood, a mahogany look-alike, is used in less expensive grades of furniture; it is often sold as Philippine mahogany. The wood varies in color from tan to brown to dark red, with a ribbonlike grain pattern similar to that of true mahogany. It is open-grained, with a coarser texture than that of mahogany, and is usually filled. Lauan requires extensive sanding before finishing; its workability is average. Red lauan is more expensive than white.

Mahogany (New World mahogany, African mahogany). This hardwood is a traditional favorite for fine furniture, one of the most treasured furniture woods in the world. It's also used extensively in veneers. Mahogany varies in color from medium brown to deep red-brown and dark red; the grain is very distinctive and attractive. The wood is open-grained, and is usually filled before finishing. Mahogany should not be bleached or stained, although it is occasionally stained to a walnut color. Mahogany is easy to work with hand tools. It is very expensive.

Gum

Hickory

Lauan

Mahogany

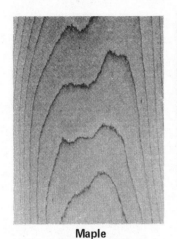

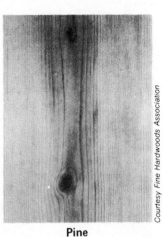

Maple

Oak

Pecan

Pine

Courtesy Fine Hardwoods Association

Courtesy Fine Hardwoods Association

Courtesy Fine Hardwoods Association

Courtesy Fine Hardwoods Association

Maple (sugar maple). Maple is a strong, dense, attractive hardwood, used in furniture and for butcher blocks. Its color is light brown, with a reddish cast; the grain is usually straight, but also occurs in bird's-eye, curly, or wavy patterns. Maple is close-grained, and does not require a filler; it should not be stained. Maple is difficult to work with hand tools, and is usually expensive.

Oak (white oak, red oak). This abundant hardwood has always been valued for its strength and its attractive grain; it is used extensively for solid furniture and, in modern furniture, for veneers. White oak is a rich grayish brown color; red oak is similar, but with a pronounced reddish cast. Both types of oak are distinctively grained, with prominent rays or streaks. The wood is open-grained and is almost always filled, although it can be left unfilled. Oak is attractive either unstained or stained. The wood is very hard, and is difficult to work with hand tools. It is moderately expensive; red oak is usually less expensive than white.

Pecan. This southern hardwood is quite strong, and is used extensively in dining and office furniture; pecan veneers are also common. The wood varies from pale brown to reddish brown, with some dark streaks; the grain is quite pronounced. Pecan is close-grained, and does not require a filler; it is often stained to a darker color. The wood is difficult to work with hand tools; the price is moderate.

Pine (white pine). This softwood was used extensively for Colonial furniture, and is one of the basic woods of modern furniture; it's used in almost all types of furniture, and is the primary wood used for unfinished furniture. The wood varies from cream to yellow-brown, with clearly marked growth rings; it is close-grained, so no filler is required. Pine is almost always stained to give it character and accentuate the grain. It is light and soft, and very easy to work with hand tools; it is inexpensive.

Poplar (yellow poplar). Poplar is a moderately soft hardwood, used in inexpensive furniture and in combination with more expensive woods. The wood is brownish yellow, with a distinctive green tinge; the grain is subdued. Poplar is close-grained, so no filler is required. It stains very well; it is almost always stained to give the wood character, and can be stained to look like walnut, cherry, or oak. Poplar is relatively light, and is easy to work with hand tools. It is inexpensive.

Redwood. This distinctive softwood is used primarily for outdoor furniture; it is resistant to decay and insects, and is rarely finished. The wood is a deep reddish brown, with well-marked growth rings; it is close-grained, so no filler is required. Redwood should not be stained, and is usually left unfinished. It is moderately hard, and is easy to work with hand tools; its price varies regionally.

Rosewood (Brazilian, Indian, or Ceylonese rosewood). This hardwood, like mahogany, is one of the finest and most valued furniture woods; it's also used for veneers. Rosewood varies in color from dark brown to dark purple, with rich, strongly marked black streaks. The wood is open-grained, and should be filled before finishing; it should not be stained. Rosewood is difficult to work with hand tools, and is very expensive.

Satinwood (East Indian satinwood). Satinwood has always been prized for fine hardwood veneers and also for use in decorative inlays and marquetry. Its color varies from bright golden yellow to a darker yellowish brown, with a very distinctive and attractive mottled or ribbon-striped pattern. The wood is close-grained, and does not require a filler. Satinwood should not be bleached or stained, and should be treated very gently.

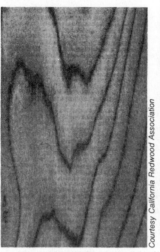

| Poplar | Redwood | Rosewood | Satinwood |

Courtesy Forest Products Laboratory
Courtesy California Redwood Association
Courtesy Fine Hardwoods Association
Courtesy Fine Hardwoods Association

Satinwood is fairly easy to work with hand tools. It is very expensive.

Sycamore. This hardwood is used extensively in inexpensive furniture and in veneers; it is very resistant to splitting, and is also a favorite wood for butcher blocks. The wood varies from pinkish to reddish brown in color, with prominent, closely spaced rays; the grain pattern is distinct. Sycamore is close-grained, so no filler is required. It is very seldom stained. Sycamore bleaches well. It is moderately easy to work with hand tools, and moderately priced.

Teak. Teak is one of the choice furniture hardwoods, and has traditionally been used for both solid pieces and veneers. Teak varies from rich golden-yellow to dark brown, with dark and light streaks. The wood is open-grained, and should be filled before finishing; it

should not be stained. Teak is usually finished with oil. Teak is both hard and heavy, and can be difficult to work with hand tools. It is very expensive.

Walnut (black walnut, European walnut). Walnut has traditionally been used for fine furniture, and is still in demand today; it is commonly used in veneers. Walnut is chocolate brown, sometimes with dark or purplish streaks; its grain is very striking and attractive. The wood is open-grained, and is usually filled; it should not be stained. Walnut is both hard and heavy, and is easy to work with hand tools. It is very expensive.

Other Woods. Although most furniture is made with the woods listed above, many other woods are sometimes used in furniture construction. Some of the other woods sometimes used for furniture are alder, apple, aspen, chestnut, cottonwood, cypress, fir, hackberry,

| Sycamore | Teak | Walnut | Ebony |

Photos Courtesy Fine Hardwoods Association

| Lacewood | Avodire | Elm Burl | Bird's-Eye Maple |

hemlock, holly, koa, laurel, locust, magnolia, pearwood, spruce, tupelo, and willow. Treat all wood according to its apparent traits.

Veneer and Inlay Woods. Some rare woods are used specifically for fine veneers and inlays. Veneers and inlays are often cut from trees with unusual or very distinctive growth patterns: crotch, burl, and butt cuts are common. Fine veneers are often cut from bird's-eye maple, carpathian elm burl, crotch and fiddleback mahogany, makori, striped sapele, roped avodire, gum burl or butt, dappled walnut, walnut stumpwood, ebony, and lacewood. Commonly used inlay woods include ebony, harewood, holly, laburnum, mulberry, orientalwood, pheasantwood, rosewood, satinwood, thuya burl, tulipwood, walnut, yew, and zebrawood.

THE DECISION: IS IT WORTH SAVING?

With any piece of furniture, the practicality of refinishing eventually comes down to one question: is it worth saving? Once you've found a piece you like, and decided what it is, look at it again to see what kind of shape it's in. Most old furniture is fairly sturdy, or it wouldn't have survived; but chances are it's also taken a beating over the years. Are the legs even? Is the piece sturdy? Does it wobble? Do doors and drawers work properly? Are the joints well made, and have they separated?

Assess the amount of work you'll have to do to restore the piece. Is hardware complete and tight? Are hinges adequate? Are drawer guides or dust panels missing? Is the wood covered with many coats of paint? If the piece of furniture is in fairly good condition, or if it's definitely an antique, it will be worth your time and effort to refinish. If the wood is broken or badly damaged, there are parts missing, or the joinery is in-

ferior, don't waste your time unless the piece is an antique.

How bad does the damage have to be before it makes refinishing impractical? This depends on how much work you're willing to do, but there are a few guidelines for decision-making.

First, look for dry rot or insect damage. Dry rot cannot be repaired; the rotted component must be replaced, and this is a custom job. Insect damage, if the entire piece of wood is not affected, can sometimes be repaired; if this is the problem, restoration may be worth the effort. To check for dry rot and insect damage, push an ice pick or a knife blade into the wood. If there's little or no resistance, the wood is damaged.

Broken parts are sometimes repairable, but not always. If a part is split or wobbly, it can probably be repaired quickly. If it's broken off flush at the joint, the job is more difficult, because a replacement part must usually be custom-made to match the rest of the piece. This can involve expensive equipment or a professional woodworker, and the piece of furniture may not be worth the cost or the effort.

On veneered pieces, the condition of the veneer is very important. Has the veneer separated from the base, or is it damaged? Are there big pieces missing? Separated veneer is easy to reglue if it's intact, but replacing damaged or missing veneer can be expensive. If a large section of veneer must be replaced, the cost may be prohibitive.

If the piece is structurally sound, don't be discouraged by repairable problems. Wobbly joints can be reglued; missing hardware can be replaced. Coats and coats of old paint, lacquer, or shellac may be concealing beautiful wood—walnut, cherry, oak, birch, maple. If you like the piece, if it's worth saving, and especially if it's an antique, refinishing is worth all the time and patience you'll put into it.

Chapter 2

The Basics: Getting Ready to Work

If you plan on doing a lot of furniture work, it's a good idea to set up a special work area, and to stock it with the necessary tools and materials. The time you spend in this preparatory stage is well worth it; you'll have your furniture where you can work on it, and eliminate the need for last-minute runs to the hardware store. There's no need to buy everything at once—start off small, with the basic tools and materials, working your way up as you experiment with different projects. Once your work area gets to the point where you're comfortable with it, you'll find that you're doing more refinishing and repairing, and that you thoroughly enjoy doing it.

THE WORKSHOP

Before you can really start to work, you need a workshop—a place designed to meet the demands of furniture refinishing and your own comfort. Set aside a heated area in the basement, attic, garage, or utility room for working—some place where you can leave furniture undisturbed over a period of days. The furniture will need a constant temperature over 70° F, and a relatively dust-free environment. Make sure the area is well ventilated, well lighted, and enjoyable to work in.

There's not much of a way to get around the minimum heat requirement. Finishes and glues simply will not work properly in a cooler environment. A radiant space heater—not a blower type—might be a good way to turn an unheated area into a refinishing workshop. The temperature must also be constant while you're refinishing.

There are a few ways to eliminate the dust problem. First of all, choose a location away from a laundry area and away from the register of a forced-air heating system. If your home is equipped with forced-air heat,

make sure you change the filters before starting a refinishing job. You can also install a homemade aluminum diffuser across the register to spread the air flow throughout the room. Simply place a long piece of sheet aluminum over the register; elevate it with wood blocks if it stops the heat flow. The amount of time and trouble spent in clearing the dust from your work area will pay off handsomely in a dust-free refinishing job.

Ventilation is the most important safety factor in your work area, considering the chemical irritants in finishes and strippers. Cross-ventilation—air from two windows or a door and window or two doors—is best. If this can't be done, install a ventilating exhaust fan in a window; a small, inexpensive two-speed fan is adequate.

A work table should be placed in the shop area so you can walk freely around the table—no obstructions. It is important for you to work without having to turn the furniture on the table. And, since furniture is upright instead of flat, the height of the table, plus the height of the furniture piece, should be planned so you don't have to stoop, bend, or reach to the work.

Set up a work table especially for furniture repair. Standard workbenches (38 to 42 inches) are usually too high. What you need is a 4 × 4-foot piece of ¾-inch-thick plywood (A-C exterior grade) supported at each end by a sawhorse. Make your own sawhorses with sawhorse brackets, available at many home center and hardware stores. The brackets are inexpensive and tailor-made for 2 × 4's that are inserted into the brackets for legs and cross-members. Cut the 2 × 4 legs so that the height of the work table will be from about 30 to 32 inches. The proper cutting measurements will probably be on the brackets; for a 30-inch table, the legs are usually cut to 28 inches. This 30-inch measurement is, of course, an average measurement. Take a couple of minutes to experiment with the height until you're comfortable with it.

Cover the tabletop with a piece of old carpeting. Tack the carpeting to the plywood so it doesn't slide, and change the carpeting when it becomes encrusted with sawdust, shavings, and finishing material spills. The carpeting helps protect the furniture from scratches while you're working on it.

Install a locking cabinet in your work area to provide a secure, childproof spot to store finishing and repair materials. Besides security, the cabinet provides valuable storage space—a spot to organize equipment and supplies. Add a couple of shelves close to the work table to get the clutter out from under your feet and promote organization while you work.

Finally, make sure your work area is comfortable. If you feel at home there, you'll want to work there.

TOOLS

Furniture repair and refinishing jobs are jobs for hand tools. Certain power tools will make the work go faster and easier, but learn how to use the hand tools first.

The only exception to this would be a portable electric variable-speed drill. With this power tool, you can make fast work of drilling holes in almost any material. Many drills are available with a large variety of accessories: saws, grinders, lathes, and the like. Buy the accessories as you need them. Start out with the basic drill and an assortment of drill bits.

One final word on buying tools: buy *quality* tools. Buy them all at once or one tool at a time, as your budget permits. Cheap tools are a waste of money and can cost you plenty in miscut and poorly cut materials. Cheap tools can also be dangerous because they don't hold a sharp cutting edge, and dull tools can slip.

Quality tools are well balanced, carefully machined, expertly matched, and properly heat-tempered. With some care, quality tools will last you a lifetime. The cost difference between a quality tool and a cheap tool is just a matter of a few dollars.

Buying quality tools involves a little comparison shopping. Most home center and hardware stores have a "good, better, and best" tool display. You can easily spot the difference between a quality tool and a cheap tool by simply comparing one with the other. A quality tool will be well machined and look it. Cheap tools look like they came out of a poorly formed mold. The metal will be rough and sharp, or, at best, sometimes filed smooth along the sharp parts.

Primary Tools

Listed below are the basic tools for furniture projects. If your budget permits, buy them all at the outset. If not, your primary selection should include scrapers, a hammer, a hacksaw, screwdrivers, a utility knife, a craft knife, and three sizes of clamps.

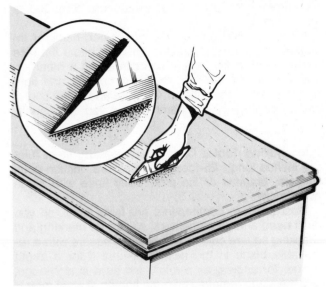

A flat scraper blade can be used to remove old finish and to smooth stripped wood. Sharpen the blade with a smooth-cut file as soon as the edge gets dull.

Scrapers: Putty knife, pull scraper, pull scraper blade, smooth-cut file, glass, rubber spatula.

A stiff-bladed putty knife can be used as a scraper in cramped quarters, and helps in application of wood filler. A pull scraper removes old finish fast—right down to the bare wood. A furniture scraper is made for furniture; it's sold primarily at furniture specialty stores. If you can't find one, buy a regular flat scraper blade; it will work fine. Be sure you keep the scrapers sharp at all times with a smooth-cut file. Scraper edges become dull fairly quickly; you'll probably have to resharpen them two or three times during a refinishing project.

Glass can substitute for a scraper, and it makes a wonderful tool for removing finish and smoothing wood. Simply buy a single pane of glass and break it as you need it. However, wear gloves and be extremely careful with glass.

A flat rubber kitchen scraper is one of the most useful scrapers for removing paint from curved and rounded surfaces, and can be used even on delicate carvings. For even greater utility, buy both wide and narrow rubber spatulas.

Hammers: 13-ounce claw hammer, ball-peen hammer, rubber or wooden mallet (or both).

A 13-ounce claw hammer is easier to swing than a standard 16-ounce hammer. Generally, you don't need the extra whacking power the heavier hammer provides, and the smaller hammer can also go into tighter quarters. A ball-peen hammer is designed for metal work; one end of the hammer head is rounded for flattening rivets. The soft faces of a rubber or wooden mallet are designed for driving chisels, and you will also need them to tap wooden furniture components into position.

If you can find one, buy a cross-peen hammer instead of a 13-ounce hammer. This tool has a flat face for heavy pounding where you can swing a hammer, and a smaller peen face to use in corners and tight quarters. Most tool outlets (hardware and home center stores) don't carry this hammer, but you can usually order it.

Measuring Tools: Combination square, steel ruler (24 inches long), 25-foot tape measure, friction-point calipers, bradawl or ice pick, utility knife with blade assortment.

Most furniture components are fairly small, so you don't need a large carpenters' square for marking and checking square cuts. A combination square with a removable blade is the best tool—use it for a depth gauge, for angles, as a ruler, and as a straightedge, with the blade removed from the handle. A steel ruler is needed for a straightedge more than for measuring. The markings, however, will be helpful.

Friction-point calipers are used to determine sizes of rounds (dowels and turnings), and they will save you plenty of time trying to match components.

The bradawl (or ice pick) and utility knife are used to mark cuts on furniture. Do *not* use a pencil; the pencil point quickly wears flat, resulting in inaccuracy. You can easily see a light knife cut or scratch line from the point of a bradawl, and you get perfect accuracy into the bargain.

A 25-foot flexible steel tape measure with a wide blade is tops for general measurements (rough materials, for example). The wide blade is stiff so you can pull out a fairly long length of tape without its bending and/or drooping.

Saws: Hacksaw, backsaw or cabinet saw, coping saw or fretsaw.

Although a hacksaw is designed for metal, it can accurately cut small pieces of wood. The thin blade makes a narrow saw kerf—a big advantage. And a hacksaw can be used for enlarging screw slots (or making new screw slots), and for cutting spring wire, bolts, nails, screws, and other metal parts.

A backsaw or cabinet saw is especially designed for cabinetmaking. It's the tool to use for making wood joints, cutting miters, and other fine, accurate work. Buy a backsaw or cabinet saw with 14 to 16 teeth per inch; the saw should be from 10 to 12 inches long. Both saws are designed for cutting across the grain of wood. However, they may be used for "ripping" (cutting with the grain), since most furniture pieces are not large enough for a ripsaw, the standard ripping tool.

For scrolls, holes, and other intricate cuts, the best tool is a coping saw. You can buy a variety of blades for this saw: rough, medium, and fine blades; blades for metal and plastic. By adjusting pins in the saw frame,

you can change the angle of the blade to cut 90-degree corners without removing the saw from the material. Its power tool counterpart is a saber saw or portable electric jigsaw.

Chisels: Assortment of butt chisels, firmer chisel, in-cannelled and out-cannelled gouges.

For all-around use, an assortment of butt chisels (⅛-, ¼-, ½-, and ¾-inch-wide blades) is the best buy. You should also have one firmer chisel with a ½-inch beveled edge. This tool goes into corners that a butt chisel can't reach. In- and out-cannelled gouges are really chisels; they're called gouges because they're rounded in cross-section. You'll use these gouges for smoothing and hollowing inside and outside curves.

Any chisel should be driven with the butt of your hand, a rubber hammer, or a wooden mallet. Never use a metal hammer to drive a chisel; a metal hammer will smash the chisel handle.

Planes: Smoothing plane, block plane.

A smoothing plane is best used for smoothing and squaring wood with the grain. You'll need this tool to match and cut furniture joints. You can also use it to unstick doors and windows, and for other household chores. A block plane is designed to cut and smooth across the wood grain, such as the end of a board.

Screwdrivers: A four-piece assortment of standard slot screwdrivers and Phillips-head screwdrivers will handle most screw driving and drawing jobs furniture repair/refinishing has to offer.

Screwdrivers are for screws. Do *not* use them to open cans, as marking tools, or for drills. And don't hit the handles with a hammer in an attempt to loosen a tight screw.

Drills: Hand-crank drill and/or variable-speed electric drill; assortment of drill bits and countersinks; screwdriver attachment.

Since most holes in furniture are small, you won't need a regular ratchet hand brace. A hand-crank drill provides plenty of capacity (usually) for most furniture jobs. Drill bits should range in size from ¹⁄₁₆ inch up to ¼ inch. You should also have small and medium-size countersinks for flathead screws. Counterboring dowel plugs can be done with a drill bit.

If your budget permits, buy a variable-speed electric drill and drill assortment in addition to the hand-crank drill. The variable speed lets you start drilling slowly and then increase the drill RPMs as the drill catches in the wood or other material. With an attachment, you can drive and draw screws—a super tool if you have lots of drawing and/or driving to do.

Clamps: Several sizes of C-clamps, strap clamp, bar clamps.

Clamps are a must for furniture repair; you will prob-

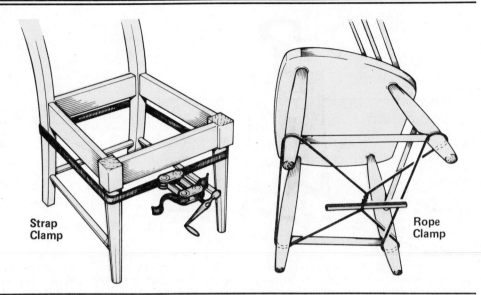

A strap clamp (left) is especially useful for joint repairs; a buckle device tightens it to the required pressure. As a substitute, use rope (right), twisted and held to the necessary tension with a stick or dowel.

Strap Clamp

Rope Clamp

ably use clamps more than any other tool. Fortunately, clamps are inexpensive (except wooden hand screws) so you can probably afford a good assortment.

C-clamps look like large letter C's with a turnscrew at the bottom of them, hence "C-clamps." You can buy them in lightweight aluminum or heavier steel. To start out, buy six C-clamps, two of each size you choose.

A strap clamp is a strap with a buckle device on the ends of it. You can use this clamp to hold irregular surfaces together. Rope may be substituted for a strap clamp, but you can't get pressure from rope unless you wedge a stick between two strands of the rope, twisting the rope tight. This isn't always possible in a restricted work area.

Bar clamps are steel bars with clamping devices on each end. It's more economical to buy bar clamp fix-

tures that fit on the ends of standard galvanized steel water pipe. The length of the clamp is determined by the length of the pipe.

Sanding Tools: Padded sanding blocks, foam blocks, dowel or garden hose.

On most surfaces, use a block of scrap wood padded with a piece of thick felt; on curved surfaces, wrap the sandpaper around a thick piece of foam. Commercial rubber sanding blocks are made with metal teeth to hold the paper in position, and may be easier to use. On concave curves, wrap sandpaper around a piece of dowel the same diameter as the curve; or slit a piece of rubber garden hose and wrap the paper around it, with the ends held in the slit. The rotary sanding attachment of an electric drill can be used on hard-to-get-at areas;

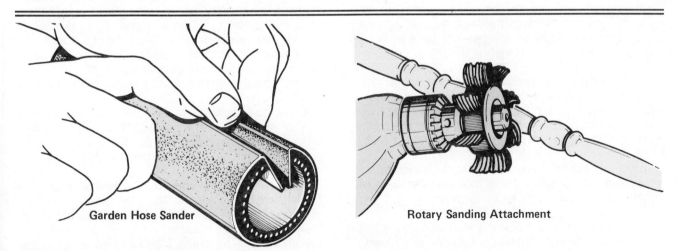

Garden Hose Sander

Rotary Sanding Attachment

To sand concave curves, slit a piece of garden hose (left) and wrap sandpaper around it, with the ends folded into the slit. On hard-to-reach areas, the rotary sanding attachment of an electric drill (right) makes a good smoothing tool; it uses thin strips of sandpaper on a rotating head.

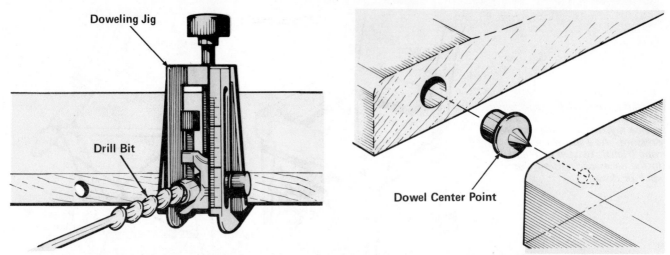

The doweling jig (left) is used in repairing joints and flat parts, where dowels are inserted to hold the parts together. The jig clamps against the edge of the part to be doweled; an adjustable sleeve guides the drill bit into the wood. Dowel center points (right) can also be used to mark the drilling location for the second hole, but they are less accurate and harder to use.

it uses thin strips of sandpaper to smooth rough spots without flattening the wood. Do *not* use a wire brush or sanding disc attachment.

Glue Injector. The glue injector, used to force glue into loose furniture joints, looks and works like a hypodermic syringe. It can save you a lot of time and trouble with joint repairs.

Doweling Jig or Dowel Center Points. These tools are also used for repairs, for doweling joints and flat components. The doweling jig is a clamp-like device that fits against the edge of a part; it has an adjustable sleeve to accept a drill bit. The doweling jig is used where dowel holes must be drilled into both joining parts. Dowel center points, small points used to mark the drilling location, can also be used, but they do not guide the drill bit; it's much harder to align the dowel holes. A doweling jig is more expensive, but if you'll be doing much repair work, it's worth the price.

Paintbrushes. For applying paint and varnish remover, throwaway brushes are fine, but for finish application, use only good-quality natural-bristle brushes. Use a different brush for each type of finish; the same brush should not be used for both varnish and shellac. Brush requirements will vary from project to project, but for most pieces of furniture, a two- to three-inch brush is best. Discard brushes if they become damaged or deteriorated, or use them as throwaways.

Lint Pickers. For varnish and enamel finishes, lint pickers are essential—these finishes dry very slowly; dust and lint must be removed during the drying period, without damage to the new finish. A small artists' brush can be used as a lint picker, but make sure the brush is

well pointed and the hairs are secure. For a better lint picker, remove the head from a wooden kitchen match or a long fireplace match. Heat rosin—music or baseball—in a pan of water; then ball the rosin and stick it onto the end of the matchstick. To use the lint picker, touch the ball of rosin carefully to the lint on the finished surface; the lint will adhere to the rosin.

Innovative Tools

Sometimes when working with furniture you may run across a problem that a standard tool or material won't solve. This is where your engineering and innovative ability comes into play. A couple of examples can get you started:

Your index finger makes a better tool to fill the edges of plywood with wood putty or filler than a putty knife or scraper. Your finger will do a smoother job; you will get a more even pressure when pressing in the filler.

A plastic playing card or credit card makes an excellent scraper to remove excess wood filler from most any surface being filled, and to clean joints and crevices.

A long nail stuck across the top edge (at the center) of a small can (like a tuna can) makes an excellent strike can, for removing excess finish from a paintbrush. Draw the brush across the nail; the excess falls into the can.

Use a salt shaker to apply pumice to a wood surface. The shaker distributes the abrasive evenly.

A good crack-filling tool is an old hacksaw blade, with the teeth filed off, inserted in a wooden handle or wrapped with electricians' tape to serve as a handle.

On carvings and other tight spots, a toothbrush or a vegetable brush is ideal for cleaning off paint remover. Use the vegetable brush on concave curves and grooves around panels in doors or drawer fronts.

The best smoothing tool to use on wet spackling compound and other wood fillers is an ice-cream stick, whittled to any shape you want.

Secondary Tools

The tools below are *not* necessary for repairs, but they can shorten your work time and offer lots of convenience. Consider buying them when you've mastered the basic tools and when your budget permits.

Magnetic Tack Hammer. This tool is fairly inexpensive, and it will perform lots of tricks: positioning a tack or nail, operating in tight quarters, providing easy-to-swing weight. One end of the hammer is actually a magnet; the driving face of the hammer is on the other end. Good magnetic tack hammers have a built-in tack puller in the magnetic end, making tack removal easy from hard-to-get-into corners. Buy the 8-ounce weight.

Jack Plane, Jointer Plane. Jack and jointer planes are expensive, but they are a must for cabinetmaking, and for extensive furniture repairing.

These two planes, with their long beds, complement one another. The jack plane is used first, for cutting and smoothing wood surfaces perfectly square. The jointer plane follows the jack plane, giving the surface a final smoothness to ready it for gluing, or for a perfect fit. These planes can also be used to rough-smooth the faces of boards, although you should probably take this type of project to a millwork shop and have the folks there run the job through a power planer.

Spiral Ratchet Screwdriver. Sometimes called a yankee driver, this tool has a push-release handle that turns automatically on a spiral shank. You just push down on the handle to activate the tip or screwing end. Several blades (standard slot and Phillips-head) are included with the screwdriver; they are usually stored in the hollow handle.

The ratchet on the shank may be set to either drive or draw screws; or you can set the ratchet in a "no turn" position. A spiral ratchet screwdriver's main role in your furniture repair life is to drive/draw a lot of screws fast. The tool can also be used for hundreds of household and automotive repair and maintenance jobs, which spreads out the cost.

Wrench Assortment. You won't need these wrenches often, but when you do they're worth the price. Various size sets are sold—from three wrenches up to a dozen or so. Sizes range from about ⅛ inch up to 1½ inches; the basic sizes are ⅛, ¼, ⅜, ½, and ¾ inch. Boxed-end wrenches are probably the best buy for furniture repairs.

Locking Pliers. With this plier tool, you adjust a little knurled knob on one handle and then lock the jaws onto almost any object. This is the tool to use for extremely tough-to-turn nuts and bolts. You can pull nails with it, too. A range of sizes is available, small to large. Small and medium sizes are adequate for furniture repair jobs.

Nail Sets. You can buy many sizes of this tool. What it does is set or countersink nailheads below the surface of wood and other materials. The cost is very reasonable, and the small, medium, and large models will all come in handy. Nail sets are tempered steel, so you can strike them with a hammer. The shank is tapered to a flat point that fits the top of the nailhead.

Dividers. This tool is used in mechanical drawing to divide a line. Dividers are also excellent tools in furniture fixing to locate screw and center points for drilling holes. You can use dividers, too, to transfer accurate measurements of various small furniture parts.

Adjustable Wrench. A knuckle-buster if you aren't careful, an adjustable wrench can be very helpful as a backup for boxed-end wrenches and locking pliers. A knurled knob adjusts the jaw so it fits most nuts; you hold it on the nut while you turn the bolt with a wrench, pliers, or a screwdriver. The medium size is adequate.

Rasp and File Assortment. There are lots of little jobs in furniture repairing that need just a touch of a file or rasp to smooth materials. This is where an assortment of these tools comes in handy. Round files and rasps are super tools to have for smoothing and enlarging holes.

Power Sanders. For fast flat sanding, an orbital or straight-line power sander is the tool to own. Its use may be somewhat limited for all-around furniture repairs and refinishing, unless you plan on restoring lots of tables, drawers, dressers, and other flat pieces. The sander should *not* be used on rounds or curves.

Orbital and straight-line sanders are the only sanders that should be considered for furniture jobs, since they don't cut fast. They have their drawbacks, however. An orbital sander uses a circular motion that can produce swirls in the wood. A straight-line sander moves back and forth; if you aren't careful, it can groove the wood.

Do *not* use a belt sander on furniture. This tool cuts very fast and can groove and ruin the wood in a jiffy, before you even notice damage is being done. A belt sander, however, is a good tool to use on a new furniture-making project where you want to remove lots of wood fast. In this case, take off the top of the wood surface with the belt sander and then use an orbital sander or sanding block to complete the fine smoothing on the job.

Another sander you may be tempted to use is the

electric drill with a sanding attachment. Resist the temptation; this can ruin your furniture.

Saber Saw or Portable Electric Jigsaw. Buy the variable-speed—or two-speed—type for cutting almost any type of material. You can buy a blade assortment for wood, plastic, metal—even concrete. The saber saw (sometimes called a portable electric jigsaw) is the counterpart of a keyhole saw, and it will perform some of the tricks of a coping saw.

Besides furniture repairs and cabinetmaking, the saber saw can be used for a good many home maintenance and improvement projects; it even has the capacity to cut 2 × 4's.

MATERIALS

Finishes, stains, fillers, and sealers vary from project to project, and deteriorate over time. If you'll be doing a lot of refinishing work, you might want to maintain a small supply; otherwise, buy these materials as you need them for each project. There are, however, some basic refinishing and repair materials that you should have on hand, and both abrasives and adhesives should be stock items. You'll use these supplies frequently enough to justify the inventory.

Paint and Varnish Remover

If you can get a discount for quantity, take advantage of it and buy a lot. You'll use plenty of paint remover for removing all types of finishes.

There are quite a few differences among removers. The less expensive removers usually contain some form of wax, may be toxic and flammable, and need to be removed with scrapers or abrasives. The more expensive ones are nonflammable and nontoxic, and can at times be removed with water. Experimentation will be your guide. Once you find a remover you like, buy a good deal of it in both liquid and semi-paste forms. The liquid is used on flat surfaces and the semi-paste on vertical surfaces, such as chair legs, where holding power is important.

Abrasives

Abrasives, the materials that work as tools, are essential in furniture refinishing and repair, but their primary role is not that of removing an old finish. Sandpaper, which used to play a major role in furniture stripping and preparation for finishing, has been replaced in part by a variety of chemicals and milder abrasives. Many professionals use sandpaper regularly, but some pro-

Sandpaper

Grit	Grit Number	Grade	Papers Available[1]	Uses
Coarse	40	1½	F,G,S,E	For initial rough sanding, smoothing rough surfaces, paint and varnish
	50	1	F,G,S,E	removal; some pros believe 40-grit is too rough for wood. Emery paper
	60	½	All papers	is used only for metal.
Medium	80	0(1/0)		For intermediate sanding, removing debris of rough sanding, preparing
	100	00(2/0)	All papers	wood for fine sanding. Emery paper is used only for metal.
	120	3/0		
Fine	150	4/0	All	For final sanding (usually) before application of stain/filler/finish.
	180	5/0	papers	Emery paper is used only for metal.
Very fine	220	6/0	G,A,S	Some pros use very-fine-grit paper as the last step in wood preparation.
	240	7/0	A,S	Otherwise, used for light sanding between finish coats (between stain
	280	8/0	A,S	and varnish, for example).
Superfine	320	9/0	A,S	Used for delicate sanding between finish coats, and for final sanding
	360	—[2]	S	of finish.
	400	10/0	S	

[1]F=flint, G=garnet, A=aluminum oxide, S=silicon carbide, E=emery
[2]No grade designation

fessional refinishers never use sandpaper, substituting steel wool and abrasive powders instead.

Sandpaper can theoretically be used for every step of refinishing, but you may prefer to use sandpaper for coarse work, steel wool for stripping and fine work, and pumice or rottenstone for finishes. The only way to decide is experimentation and experience.

Sandpaper. Sandpaper is made in a variety of types, both organic and inorganic. The organic types include flint paper and garnet paper, inexpensive papers that tend to wear down fast. The inorganics, or synthetics, include aluminum oxide and silicon carbide papers, which cost more but last longer; they're available in much finer grits than are flint and garnet paper. Emery paper, used on glass or metal, should not be used on wood; use it only to clean furniture hardware.

Some professionals use only the synthetic papers (aluminum oxide and silicon carbide), while others believe the less expensive organic papers—especially garnet paper—are sufficient for all refinishing/repair needs. One thing is certain: flint paper, although the least expensive, wears down fast, and will cost you more in the long run. Use flint paper on gummy surfaces, where any sandpaper becomes ineffective quickly. On other surfaces, the more expensive synthetic papers are faster-cutting and easier to use than the organics.

To see whether the synthetics are worth the money, start out with garnet paper and then do your next finishing job with a synthetic paper. If there's a big difference, you may feel the more expensive synthetics are worth the price; if not, you may go back to garnet paper. Use sandpaper of the type and grit appropriate for the job, as detailed in the accompanying sandpaper chart.

Steel Wool. Steel wool, in grades from medium to superfine, has assumed a major position in furniture work for smoothing and for removing finishes softened by paint remover. Steel wool is especially useful for veneers or delicate inlays, where the surface being refinished is very thin, and could be damaged by sandpaper. The one area where it can't compete with sandpaper is in smoothing down a rough surface. Steel wool does have its disadvantages: some professionals feel that steel wool gums up too quickly, and that it leaves too many steel particles behind. Use steel wool of the appropriate grade for the job, as detailed in the accompanying steel wool chart.

Abrasive Powders. For the very fine sandings of applied finishes, and for certain surface repairs, pumice and rottenstone powders are widely used. Pumice, available in grades F through FFF, is a bit coarser than rottenstone; both are useful for final finish smoothing and for stain removal. Start with rottenstone; if this is too mild, move on to pumice.

Steel Wool

Type	Grade	Uses
Medium	1	Coarsest grade for furniture work. With chemical paint and varnish remover, used to remove finishes.
Medium fine	0	Used with paint and varnish remover to rub spots off finish in final stripping stages.
Fine	00	Used to prepare wood for finishing; can also be used to dull a shiny finish.
Extra fine	000	Used as an abrasive between finish coats; also used to remove stains from finish.
Superfine	0000	Used for final rubbing of finish. Also used to remove stains, and for buffing between finish coats.

Abrasive powders

Type	Grades	Uses
Pumice	F through FFF	Fine abrasive, used for rubbing between finish coats and for final buffing. Also used in stain removal, when applied with oil (such as linseed oil).
Rottenstone	None	Even finer than pumice; used for buffing between coats and for final buffing. Also used in stain removal.

Adhesives

You'll probably use a variety of glues in furniture repair. Much of the choice comes down to personal preference, but a few basic differences should be kept in mind. The most important considerations are water-resistance and strength. If the furniture will be used outdoors, or exposed to water, use a water-resistant or waterproof glue. If the part being repaired is structural, such as the leg of a chair, choose the glue for strength.

The accompanying adhesives chart outlines the glues most commonly used in furniture work. For most repairs, carpenters' glue is adequate—experiment to find the glue you like and get good results with. In special circumstances, use the appropriate glue for the job, as detailed in the chart.

Other Materials

Paint and varnish removers, abrasives, and adhesives are the most frequently used materials in furniture refinishing and repair. Listed below are some basic materials that are used less often. Nonetheless, you'll probably find that it's best to keep these materials on hand.

Masking Tape. Use this tape for fine-lining when you apply finishes. The tape can also be used for clamping irregular glue joints. Buy two sizes: ½ inch wide and 1½ inches wide.

Throwaway Paintbrushes. You can buy very inexpensive paintbrushes to use and then toss into the junk. This may seem wasteful, but the thinner, mineral spirits, or other solvent to clean the brush after use is generally more costly than the brush—plus the time you spend cleaning.

Use throwaways for applying base finishes and stain. Do *not* use them for applying top and finish coats of any material. The more expensive bristle brushes are necessary for final finishes; buy them as needed.

Adhesives

Type	Form	Setting Time	Dry Appearance	Uses
Polyvinyl acetate glue (white glue)	White liquid, usually in squeeze bottle with applicator nozzle.	18-24 hours	Clear	General repair work. Don't use if exposed to moisture or water. Good for nonstructural wood-to-wood bonds.
Aliphatic resin glue (carpenters' glue, yellow glue)	Yellow liquid, usually in squeeze bottle with applicator nozzle.	12-18 hours	Clear	General nonstructural woodwork in dry environment; made especially for wood. Faster setting time, slightly stronger bond than polyvinyl acetate.
Plastic resin glue	Powder, mixed with water to creamy color. Sold in cans.	18-24 hours	Clear	Strong bond for structural supports. Needs a tight fit to set properly. Water-resistant, but not recommended for outdoors; can weaken under high temperatures and humidity.
Resorcinol glue	Two-part glue, liquid and powder. Sold in cans.	10-12 hours	Brown	Very strong, water-resistant. Use for both interior and exterior. Expensive. Once mixed, good for only three or four hours.
Hide glue	Liquid, or flakes mixed with water and heated.	24 hours	Amber, brown	Traditional carpenters' glue. Liquid form easier to work with. Very strong bond. Avoid use in high humidity.
Contact cement	Light-colored liquid, sold in bottles or metal units.	On contact; cures in 1 to 2 days	Clear	Best used for veneers. Don't use for wood joints. Expensive and flammable.
Epoxy	Two parts, resin and hardener, mixed to thick liquid. Sold in tubes or cans.	5 minutes to 24 hours	Clear, amber	Extremely strong bond; should be used only to fasten metal to wood. Expensive. Must be used quickly after mixing.

Paste Wax. The hard wax is best for most furniture refinishing jobs. It is available in a variety of wood-tone colors, so you may want to buy just a neutral wax for your shop inventory and then add special colored waxes as projects specify.

Black Wire. Fine black wire is a product you'll use often for many jobs—from rewiring furniture springs to clamping splits in rounds. Get single-strand black steel wire; one roll—about 25 feet—is plenty.

Linseed Oil. Oils are used quite frequently in finishing. Since linseed oil tends to become old in the container, buy just a pint or quart of it at the outset, and add more as needed. It's good to have some linseed oil in inventory, if you're serious about furniture refinishing.

Mineral Oil. Use it for mixing pigments in furniture refinishing. At the outset, buy a small bottle. Then add more if your finishing schedule requires mineral oil.

Turpentine. A quart at a time is enough. Use it for finishing cleanup and for thinning some solvent-based finishes.

Mineral Spirits. Use it for cleaning wood, for finishing cleanup, and for thinning some solvent-based finishes. Again, a quart at a time is plenty.

Denatured Alcohol. A quart in inventory is plenty. It can be used to remove and/or test shellac finishes, and to thin shellac for sealing and finishing. Buy it as the project demands.

Lacquer Thinner. Good for removing lacquer finishes and for cleanup purposes. A quart on hand will do the job.

Wood Fillers. Wood fillers include wood plastic, water putty, shellac sticks, putty sticks, and colored wax scratch-mending sticks; spackling compound is also useful for filling rough edges. Keep a small can of neutral wood plastic in inventory, but not more; it dries out quickly. Buy wood-tone wood plastic as you need it for matching purposes. If you can't find a matching color, mix a drop or two of stain with the filler. Wood plastic has no structural strength. Before you use it, clean the wood with mineral spirits.

Water putty is sold in powder form, and mixed with water to a thick paste. It dries hard as stone, and can be shaped with cutting and smoothing tools. If you can get a discount on quantity, buy plenty of water putty; if you keep the container sealed properly, it lasts forever.

Shellac sticks, putty sticks, and wax scratch-mending sticks are available in many colors; buy them as you need them. You may or may not need spackling compound, but in powder form, it costs very little and doesn't deteriorate. Keep a small package handy for use on the rough edges of unfinished furniture.

Clean Cloths, Towels, and Sponges. You'll need plenty of these for all refinishing work.

Tack Cloths. Tack cloths are used often in the wood refinishing process. You can buy tack cloths at paint supply outlets, or you can make your own.

To make your own tack cloth, launder a white cotton dishtowel. The size should be approximately 12 × 24 inches, but this isn't critical. Soak the towel in clean water and wring it as dry as you can; then fold the towel in several layers to make a pad. Pour several ounces of turpentine over the folds and work the cloth in your hands so the turpentine thoroughly penetrates the cloth. The turpentine should just moisten or dampen the material; do not soak it.

Pour several ounces of varnish into the folds of the turpentine-dampened cloth and work the varnish through the cloth to distribute it evenly. This takes a lot of wadding and kneading, so don't give up too quickly. When you're finished, the cloth will be very tacky—not wet or damp, just tacky to the touch.

Tack cloths tend to dry out as you use them. Renew the tackiness with several drops of turpentine and varnish. Keep tack cloths in closed jars or plastic bags to help prevent them from drying out. To use a tack cloth, wipe it across the surfaces you want to clean just before you apply the finish.

Bleaches. Borrow the laundry bleach when you want to remove old stain or filler. For tougher jobs, like removing black water marks, you'll need oxalic acid crystals or powder. Oxalic acid is not available in all areas; if you can find it, buy a couple of boxes. If you want to bleach out a wood's natural color, you'll need a two-part commercial wood bleach—it's expensive, but no other bleach does the job.

Aluminum Foil. Take some from the kitchen and store it in the workshop. Foil can be used in a number of ways to keep strippers from drying out.

Rope, String, Toothpicks, Etc. When you need a toothpick for repair purposes, buy a box. Same with rope, string, and other common materials. When you need them, buy bulk; you'll probably need them again.

Wood. You won't need a lot of wood unless you're rebuilding furniture extensively, but it's always a good idea to save scraps, both hardwood and softwood. For replacing furniture components, use any piece of wood that's the right type and size—an old table leaf, a birch dowel or broom handle, an ash or hickory tool handle, an ash baseball bat, a piece of maple butcher block, an old pine board. Don't ever throw away old wood with a patina, or scraps of hardwood; even small scraps are useful for glue blocks and braces.

Chapter 3
Restoring the Old Finish

Refinishing is a long, slow, messy job. Before you strip the old finish off any piece of furniture, take a good look at it—a complete refinishing job may not be necessary. Instead, you can use a few simple restoration techniques to revive the old finish. Restoration doesn't always work, but it's well worth trying before you resort to more drastic means. Start with the simplest techniques and work up; the easiest way is often best.

FINISH IDENTIFICATION

Most restoration projects require a knowledge of the finish you're working with. If you don't know what the finish is, you could end up damaging a perfectly good finish, or wasting your time on a technique that won't work. This knowledge is also essential in repair work; determining the finish is especially helpful when you're matching one finish to another.

For restoration purposes, the only distinction that really matters is the difference among the three basic natural, or clear, finishes: shellac, lacquer, and varnish. The pigmented finishes, such as paint or enamel, are easy to identify. The only other finishes you may encounter are oil, wax, and penetrating sealers, identifiable by touch and by the absence of a high gloss. These finishes can be restored only by reapplication.

On most furniture, a clear finish is one of the basic three—shellac, lacquer, or varnish. Before you do any work on the finish, you must identify it.

First, test the finish with denatured alcohol; rub a little alcohol onto an inconspicuous finished area. If the finish dissolves, it's shellac. If it partially dissolves, it's probably a combination of shellac and lacquer. Test it again with a mixture of denatured alcohol and lacquer thinner; this should completely dissolve the finish.

If alcohol doesn't affect the finish, rub a little lacquer thinner on an inconspicuous finished spot. If the area turns rough and then smooth again, the finish is lacquer; if the finish crinkles and doesn't get smooth again, it's some type of varnish. If neither alcohol nor lacquer thinner affects it, the finish is varnish.

After identifying the finish, you're ready to restore it.

Whether the problem is dirt, cracks, discoloration, or overall wear, it can often be solved by these restoration techniques.

CLEANING

The easiest restoration process is, simply, cleaning; what first appears to be a beat-up finish may be just dirt. Over a period of years, even well-cared-for furniture can acquire a dull, sticky coating of wax and dust. In many cases, this coating can be removed with an oil-based commercial wood cleaner/conditioner. These cleaners can often dig through layers of dirt and wax. They are available at furniture stores, supermarkets, and paint stores.

Following the manufacturer's instructions, apply the cleaner generously with a soft cloth, and let it stand for an hour or two. Then wipe off the cleaner with another cloth. Repeat the process, using plenty of cleaner, until the wood is clean and lustrous—this may take up to four or five applications. Buff the clean wood lightly to remove excess oil.

If commercial cleaner/conditioner doesn't do the job, remove the built-up grime with a mild solution of warm water and liquid detergent. Work quickly, and don't soak the piece of furniture or pour the solution over it—water can cause a white haze to appear on a shellac or lacquer finish, the same haze that appears when a glass leaves a white ring on a table. When the furniture is clean, rinse off the detergent with water and then carefully and thoroughly dry the wood with a soft cloth or a towel.

Let the wood dry completely. If there's a haze on the finish, you may be able to remove it with steel wool. Buff the surface *lightly*, with the grain of the wood, with No. 0000 steel wool. Then apply a commercial cleaner/conditioner, and buff the wood lightly.

If detergent cleaning doesn't work, use a solvent—depending on the type of finish—to clean the wood. Solvent cleaning is the last resort to consider, because it may damage the finish, but it is worth a try. Use mineral spirits or turpentine on any finish; use denatured alcohol on varnish or lacquer. Do *not* use alcohol on shellac or on a shellac/lacquer mixture. Working in a well-ventilated area—outdoors is best—apply the solvent with a rough cloth, such as burlap or an old towel. Then wipe the wood clean with another cloth. Finally, apply a commercial cleaner/conditioner, and buff the wood lightly.

Detergent and solvent cleaning can also be used to rejuvenate wicker and rattan furniture; use the same techniques, but be especially careful not to use too much water. Let the piece of furniture dry thoroughly; if possible, set it in the sun to dry. If the old finish is very thin or worn, apply one or two coats of spray varnish, spraying carefully to cover the wicker or rattan evenly. Let the new finish dry for several days before using the furniture.

REAMALGAMATION: THE QUICK NEW FINISH

Reamalgamation is a grand revival technique that can make alligatored, crazed, cracked, and scratched furniture look like new. Basically, reamalgamation is the near-liquefication of a marred finish so that it dries solid and unblemished. It works like magic, it's easy, and it can eliminate the need for a refinishing job; if it doesn't work, you haven't spent too much time and effort trying.

Alligatoring, crazing, and cracking are all basically the same thing. They're all caused either by sunlight or by temperature changes, and they can all be eliminated by reamalgamation. Alligatored finishes have lots of small lines intersecting into a rough pattern; crazed finishes have erratic lines running everywhere; and cracked finishes have larger lines, or just one line, running across the surface. Scratched finishes can be reamalgamated only if the scratches don't go below the finish. If the scratches are in the wood itself, you'll have to refinish the area.

The type of finish on the furniture determines the solvent used for reamalgamation—shellac is reamalgamated with denatured alcohol, lacquer with lacquer thinner, a lacquer/shellac mixture with a mixture of three parts alcohol and one part lacquer thinner. Varnish usually can't be reamalgamated.

Before you work on the finish, clean the piece of furniture thoroughly with mineral spirits or turpentine to remove all wax and dirt. Don't work on a very humid day if the finish is shellac; the alcohol used to liquefy shellac can draw moisture out of the air and into the finish, resulting in a haze or blushing.

The secret of reamalgamation is to work fast, especially with lacquer. Start with a small area to get the feel of it; once you're satisfied with your results, go on to reamalgamate the entire finish. Apply a moderate amount of solvent with a brand-new, absolutely clean natural-bristle brush—use denatured alcohol on shellac, lacquer thinner on lacquer, a three-to-one mixture of alcohol and lacquer thinner on a lacquer/shellac mixture. Work in small sections, no larger than two feet

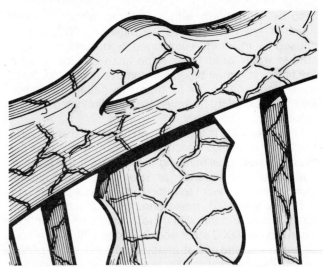

An alligatored finish, usually the result of excessive sunlight or temperature changes, shows a pattern of many small intersecting cracks. It can often be restored by reamalgamation.

square, so that the solvent doesn't dry while you're still reamalgamating.

To reamalgamate the finished surface, apply solvent along the grain of the wood in quick, long strokes; work quickly, and don't let the brush get dry. Don't try to brush out all the cracks or scratches at this point; many of them will disappear as the finish dries. If you work on individual marks too much, you may actually be removing the finish instead of liquefying it.

As the solvent dries, the finish will have a high gloss, and then, after 30 minutes or so, will become very dull. If the reamalgamation was successful, the scratches and nicks will have disappeared, and the finish will look solid.

Reamalgamation is not always a one-step process. If the cracks in the finish are deep, it may take two or three applications of solvent to remove them. If repeated reamalgamation doesn't work, the problem is probably in the wood; you'll have to refinish it.

After the reamalgamated surface has dulled, lightly buff the finish with No. 0000 steel wool, working in one direction along the grain. Don't exert much pressure, just lightly polish the finish. Then wipe the surface clean with a clean cloth. If the reamalgamated finish is very thin, clean the surface with a tack cloth and apply a new coat of the same finish, right over the old one. Let the finish dry, buff it lightly with No. 0000 steel wool, and then wax the piece of furniture with a hard paste wax. Buff the waxed wood with a clean cloth.

SALVAGING A DISCOLORED FINISH

Blushing, a milky discoloration in the finish, is a common problem with shellac-finished furniture, and can also be a problem with lacquered wood. Varnish finishes are not affected by blushing. Blushing is caused by moisture—prolonged high humidity, exposure to water, or just age. If the haze isn't too deep in the finish, you may be able to remove it with No. 0000 steel wool and oil, or by reamalgamating the finish. Deep-set blushing, however, can be eliminated only by refinishing.

When blushing is present in an alligatored or cracked finish, try reamalgamation first; this may remove the blush as well as eliminating the cracks. If the finish is not cracked, or if reamalgamation doesn't remove the blush, use steel wool to remove the discoloration.

Before you start, make sure the surface is clean; remove wax and dirt with mineral spirits or turpentine. Then dip No. 0000 steel wool in mineral oil, linseed oil, or salad oil, and rub it gently along the grain of the wood. Work slowly, and make sure the steel wool is always well oiled; the abrasive is actually removing the top part of the finish, leaving a clean finish behind. Then dry the wood with a soft cloth and polish it with a hard paste wax. If the blushing is only in the top part of the finish—and it often is—this steel-wool rubbing will remove it. Otherwise, you'll have to refinish the wood.

OVERCOATING: COVERING A WORN FINISH

Any material wears down over a period of time, and furniture is no exception. Sometimes the entire finish is worn, sometimes only heavy-use spots; worn spots are most common around doors and drawers. On an antique, wear is part of the patina of the piece, and is used to date and determine the value of the furniture; it should not be covered or restored. The same consideration applies to almost any piece of furniture: wear and tear adds a certain character. But a thin old finish can be recoated. And where refinishing is the only alternative, you may be able to repair the worn spots.

First, clean the surface carefully with mineral spirits or, for lacquer or varnish, denatured alcohol. If the entire finish is worn, clean the whole piece of furniture; you must remove all dirt and grease. Then apply a new coat of the finish already on the wood, as detailed in Chapter 6, "Applying the New Finish."

If you're touching up worn spots rather than recoating an entire finish, clean the entire worn surface; then sand the worn spots very lightly with fine-grit sandpaper. Be careful not to exert much pressure.

Once the wood is bare, it must be refinished. If the piece of furniture isn't stained, this is easy; if it is stained, you'll have to restain the bare spots to match. This isn't always easy, but it's worth a try.

To touch up the worn spot, use an oil-base stain that matches the stain on the piece of furniture; see Chapter 5, "Preparing the Wood," for staining technique. You may have to mix stains to get a good match. Test the stain on an inconspicuous unfinished part of the wood before working on the worn spots.

To touch up a worn spot, apply oil-base stain to the bare wood with an artists' brush. Finish the repair area to match the rest of the piece.

Apply the stain to the damaged area with an artists' brush or a clean cloth, covering the entire bare area. Let the stain set for 15 minutes and then wipe it off with a clean cloth. If the color is too light, apply another coat of stain, wait 15 minutes, and wipe again. Repeat this procedure until you're satisfied with the color; let the stain dry according to the manufacturer's instructions.

Lightly buff the stained surface with No. 0000 steel wool, and wipe it clean with a tack cloth. Apply a new coat of the same finish already on the surface— lacquer, shellac, penetrating resin, or varnish—over the newly stained areas, feathering out the new finish into the surrounding old finish. Let the new finish dry for one to two days, and then lightly buff the patched areas with No. 0000 steel wool. Finally, wax the entire surface with hard paste wax, and polish it to a shine.

DECORATION AND OTHER ALTERNATIVES

Restoration—cleaning or reamalgamating, spot-patching or steel-wooling—is the easiest way to make old furniture look better, but it isn't always a success. If the old finish is basically in good shape, you can often salvage a dull old piece of furniture with decorative accents or special finishing effects. If the old finish is damaged, you can cover it completely with enamel instead of refinishing. Before you remove the old finish, consider the alternatives; you may not have to refinish to give an old piece of furniture new life.

Special-effect finishing can do a lot for a dull piece of furniture. Antiquing, flyspecking, stripes, stencils, and decals can add interest and charm to many pieces, and are especially effective for country-type furniture. Where you want a bright, distinctive accent piece, an enamel finish may be the answer. Enamel can be applied over an old finish, and it hides a lot of flaws. It also lends itself well to further decoration; enamel can be dressed up with stripes, stencils, or decals, and is the most common base coat for antiquing. These alternative techniques are detailed in Chapter 7.

Chapter 4
Removing the Old Finish

There are many ways to remove an old finish, some of them more difficult than others. Shellac and lacquer finishes are the easiest to remove, requiring only alcohol or lacquer thinner and a little muscle. The tougher finishes, paint and varnish, are more common; these are usually removed with chemical paint and varnish remover. Oil, wax, and penetrating sealer finishes are less common; they are also removed with paint and varnish remover.

Unless you know exactly what the finish is and how much of it is on the furniture, you should start with the easiest techniques and work your way up—don't do any more work than you have to. If you want to paint the piece, and the old finish is sound, it isn't necessary to remove the finish; preparation involves only sanding and sealing. If you want to use a clear finish, you may be able to remove the old finish without resorting to paint and varnish remover. For any clear finish, the first step is identifying the old finish.

SHELLAC AND LACQUER: FINISH REMOVAL MADE EASY

Before you use paint and varnish remover on a piece of furniture, take a minute to test the finish with denatured alcohol and lacquer thinner. Older furniture often has a shellac or lacquer finish, but it's hard to know what the finish is just by looking. Shellac and lacquer are clear finishes, like varnish, but they're much easier to remove; the time you spend to test the finish could save you hours of work.

Test the finish first with denatured alcohol. If the finish liquefies, it's shellac; if it gets soft but doesn't dissolve, it's a mixture of shellac and lacquer. Test the surface again with lacquer thinner; if it liquefies, it's lacquer. Shellac can be removed with denatured alcohol, lacquer with lacquer thinner, and a shellac-lacquer combination with a 50-50 mixture of denatured alcohol and lacquer thinner. Stripping with chemical compounds is not necessary to remove these finishes.

Apply the appropriate solvent to a section of the piece of furniture, using an old or throwaway brush. Let the alcohol or thinner work for 5 to 10 seconds and then wipe it off with a rough cloth, or with steel wool. If the finish comes off easily, you can remove the entire finish with the alcohol or thinner; paint and varnish remover isn't necessary. Work quickly — alcohol and lacquer thinner evaporate fast. Clean small sections at a time, and change cloths frequently to keep the old finish from being reapplied to the furniture.

When the finish is off, go over the entire piece with a scraper to remove any remaining traces of finish. A furniture scraper is best; or use steel wool dipped in thinner. Always scrape with the wood grain, and be careful not to dig into the wood. Then sand the wood as necessary to smooth it. No neutralizing is necessary; after sanding, the piece of furniture is ready to be sealed, bleached, stained, or finished.

The one drawback to lacquer thinner and denatured alcohol is that they work only on lacquer and shellac. If the old finish is varnish or paint, or if there's a stain under the shellac or lacquer, you'll have to move on to the more demanding techniques of paint and varnish removers.

CHOOSING A PAINT AND VARNISH REMOVER

Most home centers, hardware and paint stores, drugstores, variety stores, and even grocery stores carry a variety of paint and varnish removers. All of these soften old finishes so that they can be scraped, washed, steel-wooled, or sanded off. There are differences among removers, however, in chemical content, removal techniques, and price.

Inexpensive paint and varnish removers soften old finishes, but they're not necessarily the bargain they appear to be. First of all, these removers may contain a waxy substance, paraffin. Paraffin gives the wood an oily look and feel and prevents the new finish from adhering properly; it must be removed with turpentine or mineral spirits before the new finish can be applied. Not only is this another step in the stripping process, but the additional money spent on turpentine or mineral spirits can be considerable. In the long run, you may

Professional Strippers

These businesses are almost always listed in the telephone advertising pages as *Joe's Strip Joint, Grandma's Strip Place,* or *Strippers A Go-Go.* What they really amount to is a huge tub of methylene chloride or other washaway chemical. Your chest of drawers, table, chair, or whatever is dipped into the solution, which eats off the old finish right down to the bare wood. The furniture item is then dipped into a neutralizing chemical and/or sprayed with water to remove the remover.

The cost of commercial finish removal usually depends on the size of the item to be cleaned; a chair, for example, would cost less to clean than a dresser. The cost for most items, however, is not prohibitive. Professional strippers will remove the finish from almost any item that has a finish, including woodwork or railings; their work isn't limited to furniture.

There are some advantages and some disadvantages to professional strippers.

Pros: *The item you have stripped comes out extremely clean. If there are several layers of finish on the* item, a commercial stripper can definitely save you hours and hours of labor. The cost is probably less to have the piece stripped than to buy the remover to strip it yourself.

Cons: *The chemicals used by commercial strippers are thought by some furniture buffs to take the "life" or "oil" out of the wood and render it "dead wood." Moreover, the chemicals sometimes soften or destroy the adhesive that holds the furniture together.*

In general, you should think hard and long about having a professional strip a valuable antique, but for run-of-the-mill furniture, thick with layers on layers of old finish, the professional way may be the easiest and best one. To help you make the decision, visit a professional stripper and examine some of the stripped furniture; discuss your project with the professional. He or she, if honest—and most professional strippers are—may recommend that you remove the old finish yourself. He might even recommend the best method and show you a couple of tricks to make the job go easier.

---

end up spending as much as you would for the more expensive paint and varnish removers.

Inexpensive removers may also be flammable and highly toxic; check the labels carefully. This makes good ventilation—preferably outdoors—a must. And you must take care to keep the area free of open flame —no smoking while you work, and stay away from appliances with pilot lights.

The more expensive paint and varnish removers probably don't contain paraffin, but they might very well contain a special wax that helps prolong the chemical evaporation process. This wax, like paraffin, must be removed after the furniture is stripped, regardless of the no-cleanup claims. A turpentine or mineral spirit rubbing, or a light sanding with No. 0000 steel wool or very-fine-grit sandpaper, will remove the wax.

Some paint and varnish removers don't have wax; while you have to take extra precautions against evaporation, the extra cleaning step is eliminated. The more expensive paint removers probably contain methylene chloride, which decreases the flammability of the other chemicals in the remover. They are probably also nontoxic, although good ventilation is always desirable.

The most expensive removers are usually labeled "water-rinsing," "wash-away," or "water cleanup." After application, the finish is washed off with water, instead of scraped or sanded off. The claims are true, *if* you follow the manufacturer's directions to the letter; the chemicals in these removers contain special emulsifiers that mix with the rinse water, resulting in a squeaky-clean finish.

The problem with these wash-away removers is that water is the natural enemy of wood and certain glues. The water used to remove the chemicals must be removed from the wood as soon as possible to avoid raising the wood grain or dissolving the glue. This water problem is especially pronounced with veneer finishes and inlays. To be safe, never use wash-away remover on veneers or inlays.

Most removers are available in liquid or semi-paste forms. The semi-paste removers contain a starch or stiffener; they're designed for vertical surfaces where staying power is important, such as the legs of a chair. These semi-paste removers are susceptible to the same problems (wax, flammability, toxicity) as the others. You can, however, buy a nonflammable, nontoxic, nonwax semi-paste. These thick removers can be used on flat surfaces as well as vertical, if desired.

For many jobs, the more expensive wash-away removers may be worth the price in time and work saved. The nonflammability of a remover is also a big consideration, and any remover that is toxic may not be worth the price you pay for it, small or large. The semi-paste removers are the easiest to work with when starting out, although you may want to experiment with a liquid remover as well. All in all, no one remover is necessarily better than another. The key to finding a remover you're comfortable with is experimentation: try different types of removers, perhaps on the same piece of furniture, until you find one you like.

Recent newcomers to the furniture refinishing scene are packaged finishing systems. These systems con-

Alternative Removal Techniques

Somewhere along the line, some helpful person will recommend that you use an easier, faster method than chemical removal. There's only one answer to this—don't do it. The usual alternatives are power sanding, lye, and heat; for milk paint, only ammonia will do the job. While it's true that these methods do work—and that professionals do sometimes use them—they can do considerable damage to the wood, and, sometimes, to you. If you don't want to spend the time to remove a thick finish with paint and varnish remover, consider having it professionally stripped. You won't save anything by using last-ditch alternatives.

Power Sanders

Power sanders remove lots of old finish very fast. If a piece of furniture isn't very valuable and has several thick layers of old finish, power sanding can be useful. Of the alternatives, it offers the least risk.

There are lots of power sanders, but only two should be considered for removing finish: the orbital and straight-line sanders. Either one of these sanders can do a good job of removing old finish from furniture, without too much danger of grooving the wood surface—if you're careful, and if you know what you're doing. Otherwise, an orbital sander leaves tiny swirls in the wood surface, regardless of the fineness of the abrasive; a straight-line sander can groove the wood.

Lye

Lye, the caustic used to open drains, is a very effective finish remover. It can also remove skin and clothing, cause blindness, discolor wood, and kill vegetation so thoroughly that nothing at all will grow in that spot, for decades. If you're ever tempted to use lye, take your piece of furniture to a professional stripper instead.

Ammonia

Ammonia is the only thing that removes old milk paint, sometimes found on antiques. It is very effective, but the fumes are very strong; it should never be used without a breathing mask or, preferably, a respirator. Ammonia also darkens wood; fumed oak has been ammonia-treated. If you must use ammonia, work outside, and keep children and pets away. Rub the ammonia on and the finish off with medium-grade steel wool.

Heat

Heat is strictly a last-resort method of removing finish, and it can very easily remove the wood, too. Two devices are available: propane torches, with special fittings to spread the heat, and electric paint removers. The electric tool looks like a small toaster element on a handle.

At best, heat has only limited utility. It can be used only on flat or slightly curved surfaces, so that a scraper can be used to remove the softened finish. It doesn't work readily on clear finishes such as lacquer, shellac, and varnish. Finally, it can be very dangerous. You may not burn the house down if you're careful, but it's very easy to scorch or char the wood. Neither the risk nor the work is worth it.

---

tain paint and varnish remover, steel wool, stain, and top finishes under one brand name. For the most part, these products are excellent, and you should check them out before starting any refinishing job.

USING PAINT AND VARNISH REMOVER

Whichever paint and varnish remover you choose, the techniques employed in using it are fundamentally the same. The basic steps are simple: after preparing the furniture, you apply the remover, let it work, and then take off both remover and old finish.

Preparing the Furniture

Before you start to apply paint and varnish remover, remove all hardware from the piece of furniture—knobs, handles, hinges, decorative locks, escutcheons, and so forth. Make a sketch of the furniture and key the hardware to it, so you'll be able to replace it correctly. If the piece of furniture has doors or drawers, remove them and work on them separately if you can—but don't force anything; if a part sticks, leave it alone.

If the hardware is clean, set it aside in order. Otherwise, polish it as appropriate. If it's blemished with paint or finish, drop it into a shallow plastic pan or bucket filled with paint remover, and let it soak while you work on the furniture. A couple of hours in the solution won't hurt it.

Some pieces of furniture may have gilded edges, special finishes in fluting, insets, and so on that you can't remove. If the special finish on your furniture will stand up to it, you can protect these areas with masking tape. Make sure the edges are pressed firmly against the wood so the remover can't seep under them.

Some finishes can be damaged by the adhesive on masking tape; the tape can pull off delicate gilding, for

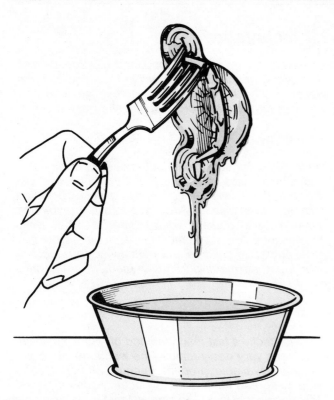

If hardware is blemished with paint or finish, drop it into a shallow plastic pan filled with paint remover, and let it soak while you work on the wood.

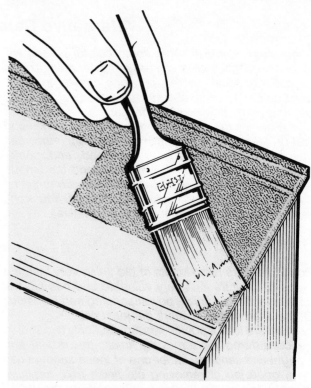

Apply paint remover liberally, laying it on with the flat of the brush to coat the surface thickly. Do not brush the remover on; this interferes with its action.

instance, when it's removed. If the finish is too delicate for masking tape, simply stay a couple of inches away from the area when you apply the remover. For further protection, tear a strip of cloth and apply the strip to the area with tape—like a bandage—to help protect the finish. Regardless of how careful you are, finishing residue always seems to find its way onto the parts you want to protect. The cloth will provide a little added insurance.

If the piece of furniture is upholstered, it probably needs new upholstery. Remove the old fabric before you refinish, and make any necessary webbing or support repairs; replace the upholstery after refinishing. Repair and replacement procedures are detailed in Chapter 10, "Structural Repairs." If you want to keep the old upholstery, it's best to remove the fabric before you work on the finish—but *only* if you're sure you can put it back on again. If the piece is large, have a professional upholsterer remove and replace the fabric.

Stripping Techniques

There are two unbreakable rules for using paint and varnish remover: use plenty of remover and give it plenty of time to work. Don't skimp on materials or on time; you won't save a thing.

Applying paint remover is a slow, sloppy, smelly job, so it's important to protect your workshop. Cover your work table and the floor around it with a thick layer of newspaper, or with a plastic dropcloth—be careful with dropcloths; the plastic is slick. Make sure you have plenty of ventilation, keep the remover away from any open flame, and cover up your skin to prevent irritation.

All removers—paste or liquid, wash-away or scrape-away—are applied in the same manner. Considering the quick evaporation of chemicals, it's best to work in small sections, say three-by-three-foot areas. It's always easiest to work on a flat surface to keep the remover from dripping off; you may want to turn the furniture piece from time to time while you work.

Apply the paint remover with a wide brush, or just pour it on and distribute it with a brush. The quality or condition of the brush doesn't matter. Lay it onto the surface with the flat of the brush, and don't spread out the mixture as you would paint—use what you think is plenty, and then add some more, coating the surface thickly with the remover. Use the brush only to distribute the remover; brushing causes the remover to lose a lot of its removal power. The chemicals evaporate very quickly; they evaporate even more rapidly when you brush the solution.

After applying a thick coating of remover, cover the

Cover the surface with aluminum foil to slow the evaporation of the chemicals; this step is especially important with removers that don't contain wax.

After 30 minutes, remove the foil and test the treated area. If you can easily rub down to bare wood, the finish is soft enough to be removed.

surface with aluminum foil to help slow evaporation. Aluminum foil is especially important for removers that don't contain wax, although it helps slow the evaporation of waxed removers, too. If you're applying remover to a vertical surface that can't be laid flat, use a semi-paste remover and try to cover it with the foil.

Wait about 30 minutes or so before testing the results of the remover—not 5 or 10 or 20 minutes, but 25 to 30 minutes or even more. Experimentation will show you the optimum time, but taking time at the outset will save you time in the long haul.

While you're waiting, apply the remover to another section of the furniture, following the same procedures. Although it almost goes without saying, it bears repeating: don't remove any old finish from areas that won't show when the piece has been restored. Once you start working on these surfaces, you're stuck with finishing them. The obvious areas are work enough; leave table bottoms and the insides of drawers alone.

After 30 minutes, remove the foil and do some testing. The treated area should by now look bubbly and cracked. Rub your rubber-gloved finger into a small part of the bubbly area. If you can easily work your way to the bare wood, the remover—and the old finish—are ready to be removed. If you can't easily reach bare wood, wait another ten minutes and try again. Paint

remover stops working, for all practical purposes, after 40 minutes. If you can't easily reach bare wood after this time, scrape away all the old finish with a wide-bladed putty knife, if you're using a non-wash-away remover; or, if you're using a wash-away, rinse off the old remover and as much finish as you can with water.

Apply another thick coat of the remover and wait again. Try the finger test again. If it still doesn't work, scrape or wash off all the old gunk you can and apply more remover. Keep doing this until you've reached the bare wood—and, once again, give the remover time to work.

Different removers require different removal techniques. Once your testing proves that the finish is ready for final removal, use the appropriate technique as detailed below, for wash-away, waxed, or nonwaxed removers.

To remove the wash-away compounds, use water and medium-fine steel wool. Do not use a scraper, putty knife, sandpaper, power equipment, or heat. It's easiest to simply hose off the furniture outside; if that's impossible, use a brush to apply the water, and steel-wool the wood clean. On curved or carved areas, use the special removal techniques listed below. When the finish is off, thoroughly dry the wood with a soft towel or other absorbent cloth. Keep in mind that water is

Wash-away compounds can simply be hosed off; if you can't work outside, apply water with a brush, and steel-wool the wood clean.

To strip slats and other vertical or round parts, apply semi-paste remover thickly; then wrap the part with aluminum foil to cover it completely.

Remove non-wash-away compounds with a scraper or steel wool; minimize the mess by dumping the scrapings into a bucket. Be careful not to gouge the wood.

harmful to wood; dry the wood immediately. Let the wood air-dry for several days before you continue with the refinishing process.

Remove non-wash-away compounds with a scraper and steel wool; scrape very carefully so you don't gouge the wood. To minimize the mess, dump the scrapings into a bucket as you work. On curved or carved areas, use the special removal techniques listed below.

If the remover contains paraffin or wax, immediately scrub the surface with turpentine or mineral spirits. Work the turpentine or mineral spirits into all the dips, dings, cracks, and carvings. Change the cleaning cloth frequently; otherwise, the paraffin or wax will be transferred from the cloth back onto the wood. The paraffin or wax should be removed now, not sanded off later.

During the stripping process, you may be tempted to change removers, especially when the remover you're using isn't doing a very good job. We agree: make the switch. But do *not* mix paint and varnish removers; follow through on the complete removal of the first chemical before you apply another one. There's no danger involved here; the mixtures may simply not work at all.

It's a good idea to treat even non-wash-away, non-

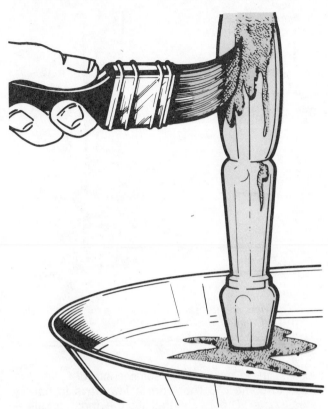

Set pie pans under the legs of the piece to catch the drippings as you work; you may be able to reuse some of the paint remover that drips off.

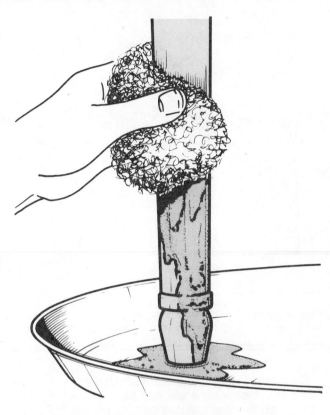

Small-diameter parts could be flattened or deformed by a scraper; instead, wipe the remover off these parts with medium-fine steel wool.

wax removers with denatured alcohol. Liberally spread the alcohol over the bare wood with a clean, soft cloth. Dry the wood thoroughly. Finally, wipe the bare wood thoroughly with mineral spirits to prepare it for refinishing.

As soon as you finish working, throw away newspaper coverings, plastic dropcloths, brushes, and cloths used to apply the paint and varnish remover. Do *not* wad waste materials up and stuff them into a wastebasket or trash can; the chemicals in the remover could cause spontaneous combustion.

Special Finish Removal Tricks

It's very easy to apply chemical finish remover to flat surfaces, but most furniture has vertical and curved surfaces, carvings, cracks, joints, and other areas that aren't as easy to work as their flat counterparts. Fortunately, pros and serious refinishing buffs have several tricks you can use to make the job go quicker.

Rungs, Rounds, Arms, and Legs. These furniture components are very hard to clean because paint and varnish removers don't stick well to their vertical or cylindrical surfaces. The trick is packaging.

Apply a very thick coating of semi-paste remover to the rung, round, or slat; then fold a piece of aluminum foil over the part to enclose the remover in a package or envelope. The aluminum foil helps hold the remover against the part, and also prevents the remover from evaporating too quickly.

The legs of furniture pieces are especially hard to strip because the remover—aluminum foil or no—will run down the legs onto your work table. The result is a mess, and an ineffective one. To reduce the mess, drive a single nail—about a 10d finishing or common nail—into the bottom of each leg before applying the remover. Set the legs in shallow aluminum foil pie pans. The nails elevate the legs so that you can remove the finish right to the bottom of the leg without lifting the furniture, and the pie pans catch the remover that drips off. You may even be able to salvage some of the remover for reuse. Be careful when driving the nails; you don't want to split the leg. The nail trick may not work if the diameter of the legs is small.

Wipe the remover off with medium-fine steel wool after the remover has properly softened the finish. Don't use a scraper or sandpaper on small-diameter components; these can quickly flatten rounds, causing all sorts of reforming problems.

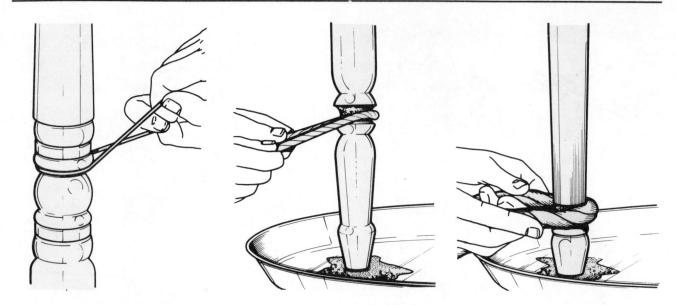

Several applications of paint remover may be necessary on turnings with crevices and joints. To remove the softened finish, use a piece of string or hemp rope (left, center); on tapers, use a thick twisted rope of steel wool (right).

Crevices, Cracks, and Joints. Use a fine twisted "rope" of steel wool, a piece of string, or a length of hemp rope to clean crevices on turnings; simply insert this string into the crevice and pull back and forth, shoeshine fashion, to wipe away the remover. For slight tapers on turnings, a thick rope of steel wool makes the best tool to remove the stripping solution.

Almost always, crevices, cracks, and joints need several applications of remover to clean away the old finish. This is because the finish tends to build up in these spots. Sometimes the crevices are so packed with finish that you don't even know they're crevices until the old finish has been removed. By removing the finish, you can actually restore the original design of the piece.

Tools for cleaning crevices and cracks also include such impromptu equipment as a nut pick, a plastic playing card or credit card, the broken end of an ice cream stick, the tine of an old fork, an orange stick, wood toothpicks, or an old spoon.

Curves and Carvings. Curves and carvings, especially shallow carvings, must be treated carefully; scraping could damage or change the shape of the wood. Clean curves with medium-fine steel wool, wiping firmly along the curve. Clean carvings with steel wool, a toothbrush, and the crevice-cleaning tools listed above; be careful not to gouge the wood. On delicate carvings, use only wood or plastic tools.

Cleanup Stripping

Even after you go through the whole chemical removal

process, there may still be some spots of finish that refuse to come off. There are a few ways to handle these spots. The best—that is, the most gentle—method is to use steel wool and paint remover on them; this technique minimizes the chance of rough spots and uneven surfaces. Sandpaper should be used when steel wool fails. Some form of scraper will fit into corners where sandpaper won't, but there is some possibility you'll damage the wood. Electric drill attachments are used by many to get the last bits of finish off, but whenever you transfer the power from muscle to electricity, you run a much greater risk of damaging the wood.

Steel Wool. Steel wool is the best way to remove leftover spots from flat, round, and all easy-to-get-at areas. Dip some medium-fine (0) steel wool in chemical paint remover and try to scrub the remaining finish off; if necessary, repeat the stripping process with another application of the remover. Once the finish comes loose, wash it off with water if it's a wash-away remover; rub it down with turpentine or mineral spirits if the remover contains wax; or, if the remover is neither washable nor waxed, rub it down with denatured alcohol.

Sandpaper. If steel wool doesn't completely remove residual spots, try sandpaper, but be careful not to leave depressions in the surface. You could conceivably use sandpaper throughout to strip the finish off the furniture, but this is a time-consuming process, and doesn't hold much appeal when compared to the chemical removal process.

Regardless of how fine it is, sandpaper works by scratching the surfaces of the wood. The final scratches are usually so tiny that you can't see them when the wood is refinished, but you should keep the scratching idea in mind; it will prevent you from using too much sandpaper too long.

Work by hand, with a sanding block on flat surfaces and a foam block on curves; sand rounds gently with the paper alone. Sand with the wood grain; sanding against the grain may scratch the wood permanently. Use medium-grit paper to remove the last traces of the old finish, and then lightly sand along the wood grain with fine-grit paper. This last fine-grit sanding should adequately prepare the wood for the finishing process, but if you don't think the wood is smooth enough, finish up the job with a very-fine-grit sandpaper.

Scrapers. Sometimes normal flat-surface techniques just can't remove the finish from hard-to-get-at areas. When this is the case, you can usually remove the stubborn spots with scrapers. Used with caution, these are very effective tools; they can easily scratch or gouge the wood, however, so be careful. Scrape tight spots between grits of sandpaper or grades of steel

If spots of finish are left after stripping, remove them with steel wool dipped in paint remover; scrub along the grain of the wood until the finish loosens.

wool, to minimize differences in texture and height between scraped and sanded surfaces.

A good sharp pull scraper fits into corners to remove finish; or use it on flats, contours, and tapers. The scraper must be used with the grain, so be sure you know the direction of the grain before you start working. Keep the blade of the scraper sharp—scraper blades dull fast, so sharpen them frequently with a smooth-cut file.

Scrapers come in all shapes and sizes: putty knives, paint scrapers, pull scrapers, cabinet scrapers, scraper blades (which are just pieces of metal with a sharpened edge), and broken glass. On some projects, you may be able to use a sharp butt chisel as a scraper; for tiny jobs, the edge of a coin can be effective. Don't overlook other scraping tools—rubber spatulas, knives, bottle caps, golf tees, utility knife blades, screwdriver tips, and your thumbnail. For some jobs, you may even find that a car windshield scraper works best.

Electric Drill Attachments. Useful electric drill attachments include a wire brush and a rotary sanding attachment—*not* a disc sanding attachment. The sanding attachment consists of small strips of sandpaper which spin around as the drill spins. Either of these attachments can be used on hard-to-get-at places when the hand-powered methods fail, but either of them can also damage the wood, very quickly. If you do have to use electric drill attachments, work slowly and watch them carefully.

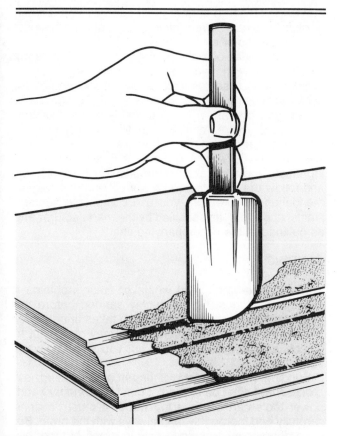

One of the best tools for refinishing is a rubber kitchen scraper; use it to remove the softened finish from moldings and other hard-to-get-at and easily damaged areas.

Chapter 5

Preparing the Wood

Refinishing furniture isn't just a matter of stripping off one finish and slapping on another; it also involves preparation of the stripped wood—sanding, sealing, filling, bleaching, staining, and repairing. Preparing the wood takes both time and elbow grease, but it's vital to the success of your refinishing job; the finish is only as good as the preparation for it. You may end up spending more time on this step than you did on the stripping—but your results will be worth the effort.

First, take a good look at the piece of furniture. How has the stripping process affected it? Are the joints loose? Do burns, stains, or other blemishes still show? Are veneers loose or bubbled? Before you prepare and finish the wood, repair the damage. Any problems you ignore now will show up all too clearly later, because the finish will accentuate the damage.

Second, look at the wood itself. What kind of wood is it? Is the grain open or closed? The type of wood determines the preparation—open-grained woods should usually be filled; some woods may need special treatment. Is the piece of furniture made with more than one kind of wood? If it is, you may have to bleach or stain the less conspicuous wood—usually the less expensive one—so that it matches the main surfaces.

Finally, look at the color and texture of the stripped wood. Is there an old stain or filler left in the wood? It should usually be bleached out. Is the color blotchy or uneven? Is one part of the furniture darker than another? Is the wood darker or lighter than you want it to be? Can you see a distinct grain pattern? With bleach or stain you can correct almost any color problem or achieve any color effect you like.

With any piece of furniture, the finish you choose will determine how the wood should be prepared. Not all finishes can be used over all sealers, stains, and fillers; not all finishes require the same amount of preparation. Before you prepare a piece of furniture for finishing, make sure you're familiar with the special characteristics and requirements of the finish you plan to use; see Chapter 6, "Applying the New Finish." Read the ingredient and application information on the container, and follow the manufacturer's instructions and recommendations. Make sure you use compatible sealers, stains, and fillers, as specified by the manufacturer and as outlined in the accompanying chart.

SANDING

Whatever the wood, and whatever color problems it may have, it must be thoroughly sanded before the new finish can be applied. This step takes priority over all other surface preparations—you may also want to bleach, stain, or fill the wood, but you should always sand it first.

Sanding, more than any other part of refinishing, is a process that can't be rushed. It must be done by hand; power tools can damage the wood. It must be done carefully and thoroughly, and always with the grain. But it's a demanding technique only in terms of time, because what it requires is chiefly patience. The care you put into sanding will determine the quality of the finish.

After stripping, examine the piece of furniture for surface and structural problems – burns, stains, cracks, loose veneer. Make all repairs before finishing the wood.

Sanding Technique

The first rule of sanding is to work with the grain of the wood, because cross-grain sanding can leave permanent and very obvious scratches. The second rule is to use a sanding block, because you can't exert even sanding pressure without one. For flat surfaces, the block should be padded; an unpadded block has no give, and grit caught under the sandpaper can scratch the wood as you work. For curved surfaces, your best bet is a thick piece of foam padding or sponge covered with sandpaper; the padding shapes itself to the curves, providing firm, even pressure.

Good sanding technique is easy to learn and apply. Using a sanding block, sand in long, light, even strokes along the grain of the wood. Don't press hard; too much pressure can cause gouging at the edge of the sanding block. Change the sandpaper as soon as it clogs or wears smooth.

To smooth the wood evenly and thoroughly, work with successively finer grades of sandpaper. The slight roughness left by the first sanding will be removed in the next sanding; the final sanding will remove the last traces of roughness. Start sanding with coarse-grit paper—grade 3/0 for most woods; grade 4/0 for very soft woods, such as pine or poplar. Work up to grades 4/0, 5/0, and finally 6/0 sandpaper. Although finer-grit paper would theoretically produce a smoother surface, sanding with too fine a paper can clog the wood and interfere with finishing.

Sand the entire piece of furniture with each grade of sandpaper before moving on to the next grade. Between sandings, brush off or vacuum up all sanding debris, and then wipe the wood clean with a tack cloth—dust or grit caught under the paper can scratch the wood. If there are tight corners you can't get at with the sandpaper, use a very sharp scraper, very carefully, to smooth the wood in these areas between sandings. Scrapers can leave gouges or scratches, so use them only when sanding isn't possible.

Rungs, Rounds, and Spindles. Narrow rungs, spindles, legs, and other round parts need special treatment. Hard sanding with coarse-grit paper, with or without a block, can flatten or deform round parts; only the minimum of wood should be removed. To sand round parts, cut narrow strips of fine-grit—grades 5/0 and 6/0—sandpaper; don't use coarser grades at all.

Compatible Finishing Products

Type of Finish	Type of Product Required		
	Sealer	Stain	Filler
Natural varnish	Thinned varnish or shellac	Any	Any
Polyurethane varnish	Thinned varnish or compatible sanding sealer	Any	Compatible (read label)
Penetrating resin	None; under stain, thinned shellac	Any except varnish- or vinyl-base; oil-base preferred	None
Shellac	Thinned shellac	Any except alcohol-base	Any
Lacquer	Thinned shellac, thinned lacquer, or lacquer-base sanding sealer	Lacquer-base, NGR, or water	Lacquer-base; if other, let dry 48 hours
Oil	None	Any except oil-base	Any
Wax	None; under stain, thinned shellac	Any; with sealer stain system, none	Any
Enamel	Thinned shellac	None	Any

Always sand with the grain of the wood, making long, light, even strokes with a padded sanding block.

To sand spindles and other rounds, wrap a strip of sandpaper around the part and pull the ends to buff-sand it.

Wrap a strip of paper around the part, crosswise, and pull the ends back and forth to buff-sand the wood. Move up and down each round, changing your angle of sanding as you work to smooth the wood evenly. Be careful not to leave horizontal grooves in the wood at the edges of the sandpaper strips.

Carvings. Carvings, especially shallow ones, must be treated carefully. Because coarse sanding could blur the lines of the carving, use only fine-grit sandpaper, grades 5/0 and 6/0, to smooth the stripped wood; work without a sanding block. Sand lightly along the grain of the wood, pressing the paper into cut-out areas with your fingertips. Sand as far down into the carving as you can, but be careful not to flatten rounded surfaces.

Crevices and Curved Edges. Sand along crevices with a strip of sandpaper, creased to fit into the angle of the crevice. Sand only along the crevice, and use slow strokes; keep the pressure even. Make sure the sandpaper doesn't slip; if you're not careful, you could damage the edges of the wood at the sides of the crevice. Sand convex curves carefully along the curve, pressing lightly with your fingers and being careful not to damage any adjoining surfaces or edges. To smooth concave curves, use a piece of dowel the same diameter as the curve. Wrap a piece of sandpaper around the dowel and push it carefully back and forth along the curve. At the ends of the curve, be careful not to slam the dowel into any adjoining surfaces.

On carvings, sand lightly along the grain, pressing the sandpaper into the carving. Be careful not to flatten the wood.

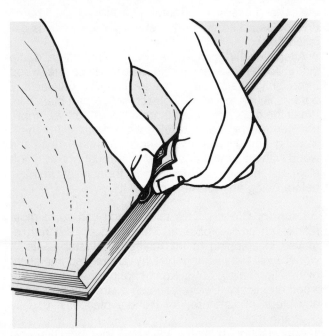

Crease the sandpaper to fit into crevices; sand carefully and slowly so you don't damage the edges of the wood.

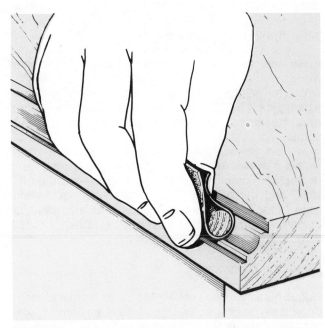

To sand a concave curve, use a piece of dowel, the same diameter as the curve, wrapped with sandpaper.

Veneers and Fine Patinas. If the piece of furniture you're working on is veneered, it must be treated very carefully; the usual sanding techniques could cause serious damage to the wood. The same thing is true for wood with a fine patina—normal sanding will remove the patina. For the best results, veneers and pieces with a fine patina should be smoothed very gently.

Smooth sturdy whole-surface veneers with fine-grit sandpaper, grades 5/0 and 6/0. Do not use coarser grades. On very thin veneers and wood with a patina, smoothing is best done with steel wool. The technique is essentially the same as for sanding; all you really need is patience.

Start working with No. 0 steel wool if the surface is rough, and work up to Nos. 00 and 000 for the final smoothing. If the surface is smooth, use only the finer grades of steel wool. Between grades, brush off or vacuum up all dust and steel wool debris, and then wipe the wood clean with a tack cloth.

Raising the Grain

When wood is moistened, the cells that make up the grain swell, raising the grain above the surface of the wood. Any liquid causes this reaction; even when the wood is smoothly sanded, the finish itself acts to raise the grain. To prevent the appearance of a raised grain in the finished piece of furniture, the grain should be purposely raised and then sanded down before the finish is applied, after the final sanding.

The simplest grain-raiser is water. Sponge the sanded piece of furniture with cold water, soaking the wood evenly and thoroughly; then wipe off any excess. The wood must be evenly wet, with no dry spots and no puddles, or it may dry with water stains. Be especially careful not to overwet veneers; the glue that holds them may be water-soluble.

Let the wood dry completely. When it's thoroughly dry, the raised fibers of the grain will stick up stiffly above the surface. With grade 5/0 or 6/0 sandpaper, lightly smooth these raised fibers down to the surface of the wood; use No. 000 steel wool on very delicate surfaces. Be careful not to roughen the surface. Then brush off or vacuum up the sanding debris, and wipe the wood clean with a tack cloth.

BLEACHING

In most cases, bleaching is essentially a first-aid measure, not a routine part of refinishing. A piece of furniture should be bleached if the surface is marked by stains, black rings, or water spots, if the wood is discolored or blotchy, if the color is uneven, or if an old stain or filler is left after the finish is removed. Old filler is often a problem with oak, walnut, and mahogany. Bleaching can also be used to even the color of a piece of furniture made with two or more woods, by lightening the darker wood to match the lighter one.

Bleach can also be used cosmetically, to lighten the color of a whole piece of furniture. This technique obviously isn't recommended for delicate inlays, veneers, or antiques, or for furniture made with rare wood, but it can be used to lighten a dark piece to match your other furniture. And as a last resort, bleaching can sometimes work wonders on a dull, heavy-looking piece.

Before you use bleach on any piece of furniture, make sure the wood is suitable for bleaching. Some woods don't accept bleach well—cherry and satinwood, for instance, should never be bleached. Some woods, such as bass, cedar, chestnut, elm, redwood, and rosewood, are very difficult to bleach, and some—notably pine and poplar—are so light that bleaching makes them look lifeless. Birch, maple, and walnut can be bleached, but bleaching destroys their distinctive color. And the rare woods—mahogany, teak, and the other choice woods—seldom benefit from bleaching. Common woods that are easy to bleach, and may benefit from it, include ash, beech, gum, and oak.

Choosing a Bleach

Not all bleaching jobs call for the same type of bleach; depending on the problem you want to correct, you may need a very strong bleaching agent or a relatively mild one. To remove ink stains or white water marks, to even a mottled surface, or to remove an old stain or filler left after stripping, use liquid laundry bleach. To remove black water marks or lighten chemical-darkened wood, use oxalic acid, available in paint stores and drugstores. Oxalic acid also usually removes old stain or filler. To change the color of the wood itself, you'll need a two-part commercial wood bleach.

Bleaching Technique

Whatever bleach you use, remember that the results are permanent—you may be able to restain if you make the wood too light, but uneven bleaching is very hard to remedy. Make sure the wood is absolutely clean, and touch it as little as possible; the bleach must penetrate the wood evenly. Before applying the bleach, test it on a scrap piece of the same wood or on a hidden part of the piece of furniture. Make sure you know exactly what the bleach will do, and how fast. In general, bleaches act quickly on soft woods, slowly on hard woods.

Bleaching isn't difficult, but it does require some precautions—bleaches are fairly strong chemicals, and the stronger ones can damage skin, eyes, and lungs. Wear rubber gloves and safety goggles when working with bleach, and make sure your working area is well ventilated; follow the bleach manufacturer's instructions exactly. If you get bleach on your skin, wash it off immediately.

Bleaching also requires careful application and removal. With any bleach, use a synthetic-bristle brush—the chemicals will damage natural bristles. Apply the bleach along the grain of the wood, wetting the surface evenly and thoroughly; there should be no dry spots and no puddles. Let the bleach work as detailed below.

After bleaching, wipe the wood clean with a damp cloth. To remove any residue, neutralize the wood thoroughly; use an ammonia solution for oxalic acid, a borax solution for laundry bleach or two-part bleaches. Wash the bleached wood thoroughly with the appropriate neutralizer; be careful not to overwet it. Then, working quickly to prevent water damage, rinse the wood with clean water and dry it thoroughly with a soft cloth. Let the piece of furniture dry for at least two days before doing any further work on it.

Laundry Bleach. This mild bleach can solve most refinishing color problems, from stain or filler not removed in stripping to ink stains and water spots. It works well for evening blotchy areas and for slight overall lightening, but it won't change the color of the wood drastically. Before you use a stronger bleach on any piece of furniture, try laundry bleach; it usually does the trick.

Apply laundry bleach full-strength, brushing it evenly over the entire surface; if you're removing spots or lightening discolored areas, apply bleach full-strength to those areas. Laundry bleach works quickly; after a minute or two, you should be able to see the stain fading. If you're bleaching out an old stain, wipe the bleach off with a damp cloth when the stain has lightened. If you're spot-bleaching to remove spots or blend color areas, wait until the bleached spots are roughly the same color as the rest of the wood; then apply bleach again over the entire surface. Remove the bleach with a damp cloth when the color is even. Finally, neutralize the treated wood with a solution of 1 cup of borax dissolved in 1 quart of hot water. Neutralize, rinse with clean water, and dry it thoroughly.

Oxalic Acid. Oxalic acid, sold in powder or crystal form, is used to remove black water marks from wood. It is also effective in restoring chemically darkened wood to its natural color—a problem you're not likely to encounter unless you have a piece of furniture commercially stripped, because lye and ammonia, the chemicals that discolor wood, are not recommended for nonprofessional use. Oxalic acid must be used on the entire surface of the wood, because in most cases it also bleaches out old stain; you may have to bleach the entire piece of furniture to get an even color. Oxalic acid is more effective in lightening open-grained wood than close-grained.

Oxalic acid is not caustic, but it is poisonous; wear rubber gloves and wear safety goggles, and make sure ventilation is adequate. To prepare the acid, mix a saturated solution with warm water: 1 ounce of powder or crystals per 1 cup of warm water. Make sure you prepare enough bleach to treat the entire surface or piece of furniture.

To even blotchy areas and to lighten the wood slightly over-all, apply laundry bleach full-strength along the grain of the wood, over the entire surface.

Black water stains should be removed with oxalic acid, brushed on over the entire surface. Then neutralize the acid with ammonia.

Apply the acid solution evenly to the wood, brushing it on along the grain to cover the entire surface. On soft wood, you'll see results very quickly; on hard woods the bleaching takes longer. Let the acid work for about 20 minutes and then wipe it off with a damp cloth. If the surface isn't fully or evenly bleached, reapply the acid as necessary—on hard woods, complete bleaching may take up to an hour. Wipe the wood clean with a damp cloth and wash it with clean water; then neutralize it with a solution of 1 cup of household ammonia and 2 quarts of water. Rinse it again with clean water and dry it thoroughly.

Two-Part Bleaches. The two-part commercial wood bleaches are used to lighten or remove the natural color of wood; if you want a dark old piece to fit in with a roomful of blond furniture, this is the bleach to use. Two-part bleach is very strong, and must be used carefully; wear rubber gloves and safety goggles. This type of bleach is also expensive. Several brands are available.

Two-part bleach is easy to use, and usually works very quickly. The two components of the bleach—labeled "1" and "2" or "A" and "B"—are usually applied separately; read the manufacturer's instructions and follow them exactly. The first solution is usually allowed to work for about 20 minutes before the second solution is applied.

Following the directions carefully, apply the first solution and let it work; then apply the second solution. One treatment usually bleaches the wood completely, but if the wood isn't light enough, treat it again. Wipe the bleached wood clean with a damp cloth, and then neutralize it with a solution of 1 cup of borax dissolved in 1 quart of hot water. Rinse the wood with clean water, and dry it thoroughly.

Post-Bleach Treatment

Treatment with any bleach raises the grain of the wood, even when the piece of furniture has already been thoroughly sanded. To prevent the raised grain from affecting the finish, it must be resanded to the level of the wood surface after the wood is dry.

After bleaching, let the piece of furniture dry for at least two days. Then sand the grain down lightly with grade 5/0 or 6/0 sandpaper; be careful not to roughen the surface. Because there may still be some chemical residue in the wood, wear a breathing mask, and use

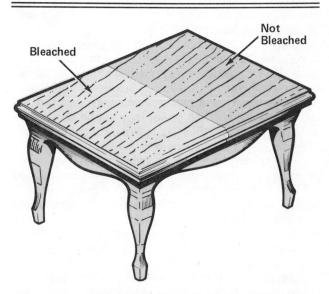

To lighten or remove the color of the wood itself, so that a dark piece matches the other furniture in a room, use a two-part commercial wood bleach.

a vacuum to remove sanding dust. Wipe the wood clean with a tack cloth.

One other complication of bleaching, especially with laundry bleach, is that the wood may be left with a whitish or grayish color. This is not serious; it indicates that the bleach has dried out the fibers of the wood surface. On hard woods, it disappears when the finish is applied. On soft woods, the gray color may be pronounced and the loose fibers obvious. To remove them, rub the wood firmly along the grain with No. 000 steel wool; rub the entire bleached area, and make sure the color is even. The grayish cast will disappear completely when the finish is applied.

SEALING

Like good sanding, careful sealing can make all the difference to your results in refinishing furniture. Sealer coats are used between finishing steps, to ensure even penetration of stains and finishes, to prevent bleeding of stains and fillers, to form a good base for the finish, and to make the finished surface smoother. Sealing is not difficult, and it's well worth the extra time it takes. For professional results, seal all surfaces before and after staining and filling, and before finishing. Some sealers have a built-in stain; the label on the container will usually specify that the product is a stain/sealer.

Choosing a Sealer

The traditional sealer for shellac, lacquer, and natural varnish finishes is thinned white shellac. This basic sealer is simply a mixture of 1 part white shellac (4-pound cut) and 3 to 4 parts denatured alcohol. Shellac is suitable for most refinishing jobs, but it cannot be used with polyurethane varnish, or with water or NGR stains. For specifics on mixing shellac, see Chapter 6, "Applying the New Finish."

Where shellac cannot be used, the easiest sealer is a commercial sanding sealer. Sanding sealer dries quickly, and provides a very good sanding base; it can be used with varnish, shellac, or lacquer. If you plan to finish the piece with polyurethane varnish, read the label carefully; sanding sealer may not be compatible with polyurethane. Sealing is not necessary before finishing with a penetrating resin sealer.

Under natural varnish or lacquer finishes, some professionals prefer to seal the wood with a thinned mixture of the same finish. To make a natural varnish sealer, thin the varnish with turpentine or mineral spirits to make a 50-50 mixture; to make lacquer sealer, mix lacquer and lacquer thinner in equal parts. These sealers cannot be used with shellac or with polyurethane varnish.

Polyurethane varnish demands special treatment. Read the labels carefully when you buy. Some polyurethanes can be thinned, with a specific thinner; with these varnishes, the manufacturer may recommend thin varnish coats as sealers. Some polyurethanes do not require sealers. If you must seal stain or filler before polyurethane is applied, make sure the sealer is compatible with the varnish. Otherwise, use a penetrating resin sealer; this finishes the wood completely, but you can apply polyurethane over it if you want a smoother finish.

Sealing Technique

Because sealers should not interfere with other finishing steps, they must be applied in thin coats. Before applying the sealer, make sure the wood is clean; remove any dust with a tack cloth. Apply the sealer with a clean brush, flowing it on evenly and quickly along the grain of the wood. Make sure all surfaces are evenly covered, and pay particular attention to any end grain. End grain that isn't properly sealed will absorb stains and finishes more deeply than the rest of the wood in a piece.

Let the sealer dry completely—about two hours for thinned white shellac; about one hour for commercial sanding sealer. Then sand the surface very lightly with fine-grit sandpaper, grade 7/0; the wood must be very smooth, but the sanding shouldn't penetrate the sealer. Remove all sanding debris with a tack cloth.

If you're applying a finish directly over sanded wood, more than one coat of sealer may be necessary to close the wood's pores completely. In this case, let the first coat of sealer dry completely before applying another coat. Very porous woods may require several coats of sealer.

STAINING

Wood is a beautiful material, but not all wood is equally beautiful. The choice woods are prized chiefly for the beauty of their color and grain; the common furniture woods are less desirable not because they don't work as well but because they don't look as nice. Antiques, whether hardwood or softwood, are often beautiful simply because the wood has acquired a patina that new wood doesn't have. In furniture refinishing, one great equalizer is used to make the wood look better: stain.

Staining is done for a variety of reasons. Properly used, stain can emphasize the wood grain, and give a light wood character. It can make a new wood look old, or a common wood look like a rare one. It can pull together a two-wood piece, restore color to bleached areas, even a surface, and change or deepen the color of any wood. Staining is not always advisable, but it can solve a lot of problems.

Before you stain any piece of furniture, take a good look at it. If it's made of cherry, maple, mahogany, rosewood, aged pine, or any of the rare woods, the wood should probably not be stained; these woods look best in their natural color. If the wood is light, with a relatively undistinguished grain, it may benefit considerably from a stain; beech, birch, poplar, ash, gum, and new pine are usually stained before finishing. Some woods, like oak, are attractive either stained or unstained. In general, it's better not to stain if you're not sure it would improve the wood.

The type of wood is not the only guideline for staining; your own preference should be the deciding factor. To get an idea how the piece of furniture would look unstained, test an inconspicuous spot—on the bottom of a table, for example—with whatever finish you plan to apply. The finish itself will darken the wood and bring out the grain. If you like the way it looks, there's no need to stain the wood; if you want a darker color or a more pronounced grain pattern, go ahead and stain it.

Choosing a Stain

Several types of stains are available—wiping stains, water stains, varnish and sealer stains, NGR (non-grain-raising) stains. Some stains are combined with a sealer, and these are usually labeled as stain/sealers. Not all are easy to use, or guaranteed to give good results, so take a few minutes to plan and read the labels.

The first consideration is the finish you plan to use. Most finishes can be applied over most types of stain, but polyurethane varnish cannot. If you want to use a polyurethane finish—and this type of finish is both good-looking and very durable—look for a stain that's compatible with polyurethane. If you can't find a compatible stain, you'll have to apply a clear penetrating resin sealer over a noncompatible stain. Varnish can be applied over this sealer, if you want a shiny finish.

The second consideration in choosing a stain is the job you want it to do. The most commonly used furniture stains are based on pigments mixed in oil or turpentine, or on aniline dyes mixed in turpentine, water, alcohol, or a volatile spirit. Other types of stains include varnish stains, sealer stains, and organic stains.

Pigmented Oil Stains. The pigmented oil stains are nonpenetrating; they consist of pigments mixed in linseed oil, turpentine, mineral spirits, or a similar solvent, and are sometimes also available in gel form. They are inexpensive and easy to apply, but unless the grain of the wood is very open, they usually blur or mask the grain pattern. These stains usually don't work well on hardwoods, but can be used for slight darkening on close-grained hardwoods, such as maple. The lightening stains are pigmented oil stains.

Pigmented oil stains are applied by wiping, and removed after the desired color is achieved. The intensity of the color is controlled by the length of time the stain is left on the wood. Drying time can be long, and the stain must be well sealed to prevent bleeding through the finish; the wood should also be sealed before application. The colors fade over time.

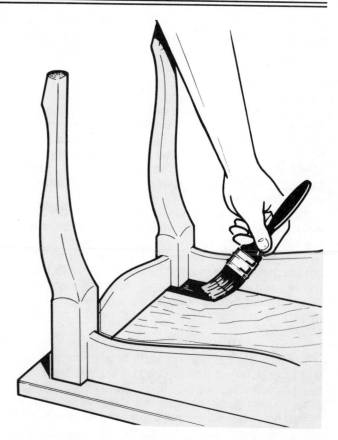

Before staining a piece of furniture, brush a little finish on an inconspicuous area to see how the finished wood looks without a stain.

Penetrating Oil Stains. The penetrating oil stains are very popular; they consist of aniline dyes mixed with turpentine or a similar solvent. They are inexpensive and easy to apply, but they tend to penetrate unevenly; for this reason, they don't work well on hardwoods, and are best used on pine and other softwoods. They can be used for slight darkening on close-grained hardwoods, such as maple.

Penetrating oil stains are applied by wiping, and removed after the desired color is achieved. The intensity of the color is controlled by the length of time the stain is left on the wood. Drying time is relatively long, and the stain must be well sealed to prevent bleeding through the finish. It is very hard to remove once it's dry. The colors are rich and clear, but fade over time.

Water Stains. Water stains consist of powdered aniline dye, mixed with hot water. They are inexpensive and produce a rich color, but are difficult to use. Water stains are extensively used by manufacturers, but are not recommended for refinishing.

Water stains are hard to apply evenly, and they have a very long drying time. They raise the grain of the wood, so sanding is necessary after staining, and color may be lost in high spots. Water stains don't bleed through the finish, but the wood must be sealed before and after staining to ensure even staining and smooth finishing.

NGR (Non-Grain-Raising) Stains. The NGR stains consist of aniline dye mixed with denatured alcohol or a volatile spirit, such as methanol. They are expensive, and they can be difficult to use. Alcohol-based stains fade over time and must be well sealed to prevent bleeding; they cannot be used with shellac. Spirit-based NGR stains don't fade or bleed, and produce a more uniform color.

Alcohol- and spirit-based NGR stains dry very quickly. Apply them with very quick, even brushing; repeated thin applications are best to minimize over-laps. One color can be applied directly over another, but too dark a color must be bleached out. NGR stains are recommended for use on hardwoods, especially close-grained woods, where oil stains would not be absorbed properly. They should not be used on softwoods.

Varnish Stains. Varnish stain is a nonpenetrating stain, consisting of aniline dye in a varnish base. It is used by manufacturers to finish drawers, backs, and other hidden parts, because it's inexpensive and no further finish is required, but it looks cheap, and is generally not recommended for refinishing.

Sealer Stains. The sealer stains are nonpenetrating mixtures of dye in a varnish, shellac, or lacquer base. Two coats are usually required, and the surface must often be protected with paste wax. No further finishing is required. Sealer stains are discussed in detail in Chapter 6, "Applying the New Finish."

Organic Stains. Several organic-base stains can be made for use on pine and other woods; the most common uses tobacco as the color, but stains can also be made from bark, roots, tea, berries, and other natural sources. These stains are interesting, but they're not recommended unless you're an accomplished refinisher.

Preparing the Wood

Before staining the piece of furniture, make sure the wood is absolutely smooth. Any surface irregularities will cause uneven stain absorption, and will result in a blotchy effect. To make sure the wood is smooth, rub it firmly along the grain with No. 000 steel wool; touch the wood as little as possible. Remove all dust and steel wool debris with a tack cloth.

To ensure even stain penetration, many woods should be sealed before staining, as detailed above. Close-grained wood may not need sealing. Thinned shellac can be used as a sealer under pigmented and penetrating oil stains; it should not be used under NGR or water stains. Commercial sanding sealer should be used with these stains. If you plan to finish the piece of furniture with polyurethane, make sure the sealer is compatible.

Apply the shellac or other sealer with a clean brush, stroking it lightly along the grain of the wood. Make sure any end grain is sealed completely; otherwise it will absorb too much stain, and turn out darker than the rest of the wood. The grain should be lightly coated but not filled; the surface should dry dull. Let this sealer coat dry completely—about two hours for shellac, or one hour for commercial sanding sealer. Then sand the surface very lightly with fine-grit sandpaper. Remove all dust with a tack cloth before applying the stain.

Mixing the Color

Whatever type of stain you're using, the most important part of the process is getting the color you want. You may be able to buy stain in the color you want, or you may have to mix colors to get the right effect. Experiment, mixing small amounts of stain and applying test batches to scrap wood, until you get the right color.

Although a wide range of stain colors is available, you can mix almost any color with two or more of the four basic shades: light oak (tan), walnut (brown), maple (yellow-orange), and mahogany (red). Most manufacturers provide mixing proportions for various effects. To dull any color, add a drop or two of black. Mix small amounts of stain at once; then, starting full-strength and thinning the stain gradually with the proper solvent, test the stain on scrap wood until you have the right color. Keep track of the proportions so you'll be able to duplicate the mixture. When you like the color, test it again on a hidden part of the piece of furniture. If the piece is made of two or more woods, you may have to mix stain separately for each wood, but this is often not necessary.

When you're satisfied with the stain color, mix enough stain to treat the entire piece of furniture. Do *not* mix brands or types of stain, and do not change brands or types in the middle of the job. It's better to have stain left over than to run out of stain with one table leg or chair arm to go.

Staining Techniques

Whatever stain you're using, it's best to go carefully. If you're not sure the color is right, thin the stain to lighten it, and apply several coats of stain until the color is as deep as you want it. Always test the stain in an inconspicuous spot, and stain the least conspicuous surfaces first. It may take longer this way to get the effect you want, but the only way to salvage a badly applied stain is to bleach it out and start over.

To prevent drip marks and uneven color, turn the piece of furniture so that the surface being stained is always horizontal. If you're working on a large piece

Brush oil stain on with a clean brush, flowing it evenly along the grain of the wood to cover the entire surface.

Let oil stain set to produce the desired color; the longer you leave it on, the darker it will be. Wipe off the excess.

and this isn't practical, start at the bottom and work up. Always work quickly, applying stain smoothly and evenly over the entire surface.

Pigmented or Penetrating Oil Stains. Apply pigmented or penetrating oil stain with a clean brush, flowing stain evenly on along the grain of the wood; or use a clean cloth or sponge to apply penetrating stain. Let pigmented oil stain set for about 10 to 15 minutes, until the surface of the stain starts to turn dull, then firmly wipe off the excess stain with a clean cloth dampened with stain. Penetrating oil stains work more quickly than pigmented ones; wipe off the excess immediately for a light color, or let it set as long as 15 to 20 minutes for a darker color.

Oil stain can be modified to some extent if you don't like the effect. If the wood is too dark, soak a clean cloth in turpentine or mineral spirits, and rub the wood firmly and evenly along the grain. This will lighten the stain, but not remove it. If part of the grain is too dark, wrap a cloth around your index finger, dip it into turpentine or mineral spirits, and lightly rub the grain you want to lighten. If part of the grain is too light, use an artists' brush to carefully apply more stain just to the grain.

Let the completed stain dry for about 24 hours. If the color isn't dark enough, repeat the staining procedure. `

Water Stains. Water stains should be used only on absolutely clean bare wood, or on new wood. Apply water stain with a new brush, flowing it on quickly and evenly along the grain of the wood; use long, smooth strokes. Try not to overlap your strokes; a double layer of stain will dry twice as dark as a single one. It's better to use several thinned coats of stain than one dark one

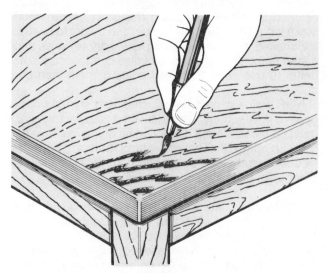

Oil stain allows some leeway for color adjustment. If part of the grain is too light, use an artists' brush to apply more stain to the lighter areas.

to minimize brush overlap marks.

Water stain cannot be adjusted, but if you're working on relatively small surfaces, the stain can be evened out by wiping. To apply water stain by this method, flow it onto the surface very liberally; then wipe off the excess, stroking along the grain, with a clean cloth. The intensity of the color is determined by the length of time the excess is left on the wood; wipe immediately for a light color, or let the stain set for a darker shade. Let the completed stain dry for about 24 hours; if the color isn't dark enough, repeat the staining procedure.

On large surfaces, apply water stain in long, smooth strokes, with as little overlap as possible; overlaps and drips will dry darker than the rest of the surface.

NGR Stains. NGR stain, either alcohol- or spirit-based, is applied like water stain, but this type of stain dries so quickly that it can be hard to apply. Use a medium-size new brush to apply NGR stain, flowing it on quickly and evenly along the grain of the wood. Make long, smooth, light strokes, and try not to overlap the strokes; brush overlap marks will dry twice as dark as the rest of the stain. To minimize overlap marks, it's better to use several thinned coats of stain than one dark one.

NGR stains cannot be adjusted, and should not be applied in very humid weather. An unsatisfactory stain must be bleached out. Let the stain dry completely before finishing the wood—about half an hour for alcohol-based stain; about one hour for methanol- or other spirit-based stain.

Lightening. Dark wood can be lightened with stain for an interesting light-dark effect. Lightening is not recommended for fine woods, because it covers the natural color and grain of the wood; but as a last resort, it can be effective. Lightening works best on open-grained wood; the effect of a lighter color is produced because the grain is filled with a light or white pigment. The lightening agent is sometimes thinned white oil-base paint, but more often pigmented oil stain.

Apply the oil stain as above, and let it set to achieve the desired effect. Wipe off excess stain and let the stained wood dry completely.

Post-Stain Treatment

Any stain, even an oil-base stain, may raise the grain of the wood slightly. If necessary, remove this slight roughness when the stain is completely dry, but smooth the wood very carefully to avoid removing the stain. To smooth wood treated with oil-base stain, rub it gently with No. 000 or 0000 steel wool. To smooth wood treated with water or NGR stain, sand it very lightly with fine-grit sandpaper. Remove all sanding debris with a tack cloth. Sanding may remove water stain in spots; if the surface is uneven in color, you may have to apply another coat of stain.

Most stains should be sealed to prevent bleeding. After smoothing the stained wood, apply a sealer coat of thinned shellac, sanding sealer, or other appropriate sealer. Do not use shellac with NGR or water stains. If you plan to finish the piece with polyurethane, make sure the sealer is compatible. Let the sealed wood dry completely; then sand the surface very lightly with fine-grit sandpaper. Remove the sanding debris with a tack cloth.

FILLING

Softwoods and close-grained hardwoods, such as maple and poplar, are ready to finish after staining; open-grained hardwoods may require further treatment. Even after the surface is stained or sealed, open-grained wood still has open pores, and a finish applied over open pores may look uneven. To give it a smooth and evenly finished surface, open-grained wood is usually treated with a filler after staining.

Whether you should fill the wood depends on both the wood itself and the finish you want. What is the piece of furniture made of? Bass, hemlock, maple, pine, poplar, redwood, willow, cedar, cypress, and ebony should never be filled; they can be finished immediately after staining and sealing. Ash, beech, mahogany, oak, rosewood, walnut, teak, satinwood, butternut, chestnut, elm, hickory, and lauan are open-grained; they are usually filled. Most of the other hardwoods—such as cherry, birch, and sycamore—are close-grained, and should not be filled.

Filling is also a matter of personal taste. Do you want a mirror-smooth finish on a formal table, or are you aiming for a more natural-looking finish on an informal piece? Filler produces a very smooth, glassy surface; if you want a more natural look, you may want to leave the pores open. This also affects the finish you plan to use. Under most finishes, open-grained woods should be filled, but if you don't want the piece of furniture to have a very smooth surface, you can finish it with a penetrating sealer, which makes filling unnecessary.

One drawback of filling is that most finishes don't bond as well to filled surfaces. In general, it's best to use a filler only when necessary, when a varnish, shellac, or lacquer finish will be applied over one of the open-grained woods listed above. If you're not sure the wood should be filled, don't fill it.

Choosing a Filler

Fillers are available in two forms, liquid and paste. The liquid type is not very useful; it's too thin to be effective on open-grained woods. Tinted liquid filler is some-

Apply filler first along the grain of the wood. Then work across the grain to fill the pores completely.

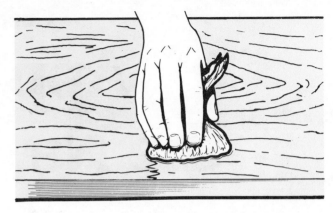

When the surface of the filler dulls, wipe off the excess with a coarse cloth, first across and then along the grain.

times used like lightening stain, to change the color of the wood. In most cases, filling should be done with paste filler, thinned as necessary to penetrate the pores of the wood. If you plan to finish the piece of furniture with lacquer, use a lacquer-base filler, or let the filler dry for at least 48 hours before sealing and finishing. If you plan to use a polyurethane finish, make sure that filling is recommended, and that the filler is compatible.

There are two types of paste filler. The most commonly available filler is based on cornstarch; it's available in a neutral tone and in several colors. This type of filler should be matched to the color of the wood; it dries only slightly lighter than its apparent color. If you can't find a color to match the wood, use oil stain to mix a filler slightly darker than the wood; check the labels to make sure you can mix it. More than one application may be required with this type of filler.

The second type of paste filler is called sanding filler; it dries transparent, and does not have to be matched to the wood. Sanding filler is silicate-based, and requires only one application. Because it doesn't have to be color-matched, it is easier to use than cornstarch-based filler.

Filling Technique

Stained surfaces should be sealed after staining to prevent bleeding; they need no further treatment before filling. Unstained surfaces must also be sealed; apply a coat of thinned shellac, sanding sealer, or other appropriate sealer. If you plan to finish the piece with polyurethane, make sure the sealer and the filler are compatible. Let the sealed wood dry completely; then sand the surface very lightly with fine-grit sandpaper. Remove the sanding debris with a tack cloth, and apply the filler.

To use paste filler, thin the paste as directed with turpentine, working it to a smooth, creamy batter. Wood with very large open pores requires a thicker consistency than wood with smaller pores. Apply the filler with a clean brush, working it firmly into the pores along the grain of the wood; then work it in across the grain. On large surfaces, fill one area at a time to cover the entire surface evenly.

Let the filler set for about 15 minutes, or as directed by the manufacturer, until the surface of the filler is dull. Then firmly wipe off the excess filler, across the grain of the wood, with a coarse towel or a piece of burlap. You want to remove the filler from the surface of the wood but leave it in the pores; you may have to experiment with the drying time to find the right timing. After wiping off the excess filler, wipe the wood slowly and carefully with a clean cloth, in the direction of the grain. Let the filled wood dry for at least 24 hours.

Post-Filler Treatment

The filled wood should look clean. If you can see a dull haze on the surface, the excess filler was not completely removed. This haze must be sanded off to prevent clouding in the finish. Sand the hazy areas very lightly with fine-grit sandpaper, being careful not to remove either the filler in the pores or stain. Remove sanding debris with a tack cloth and let the piece of furniture dry for at least 24 hours.

To prevent the filler from bleeding through the finish before bonding of the finish to the filler, seal the filled surface before finishing with the appropriate sealer. Apply a coat of thinned shellac, sanding sealer, or other appropriate sealer. If you plan to finish the piece with polyurethane, make sure the sealer is compatible; some polyurethanes may not require sealing over some fillers. If you plan to finish the piece with penetrating resin sealer, sealing is not necessary. Let the sealed wood dry completely; then sand the surface very lightly with fine-grit sandpaper. Remove the sanding debris with a tack cloth, and apply the finish.

Chapter 6

Applying the New Finish

Putting the finish on the furniture is the final payoff for all the hours you've spent removing the old finish, making repairs, sanding and staining and smoothing. The finishing step is the fun step. It may be routine; it may be creative. Either way, it is usually easy to do, if you take your time and exercise a little patience.

CHOOSING A FINISH

Furniture finishes can be classified into several basic types: varnish, penetrating resin, shellac, lacquer, wax, and oil. All of these finishes are designed to protect the wood and to bring out its natural beauty, and all of them can be assessed in terms of how well they accomplish these objectives. Consequently, choosing a finish comes down to two essential factors: how you want the wood to look and how durable you want the finished surface to be.

Of the six basic finishes, all can be beautiful, but when it comes to durability, two types outperform all the others: varnish and penetrating resin. Varnish, the most durable of all finishes, is available in high-gloss, satin, and flat forms, for whatever surface shine you want. Applying varnish can be difficult, but the results are worth the work. Penetrating resin, a relatively recent development, sinks into the wood to give it a very natural look and feel; it is very easy to apply and very durable. The other furniture finishes do have their advantages—oil, for instance, produces a very natural finish; shellac dries fast and is easy to use. But for most refinishing, varnish or penetrating resin is probably the best choice.

PREPARING TO WORK

Whatever finish you choose, it's important to know exactly what you're working with. Some finishes can be mixed, and some cannot. Each finish has its own individual application techniques; each finish requires different tools and materials. Before you can buy and apply a finish, *always* read the ingredient and application information on the container. And *always* follow the manufacturer's instructions and recommendations.

The one requirement common to all finishes is a dust-free environment during application. Providing this environment isn't easy, but it can be done. Consider using a finish that dries with a matte or flat surface; this type of finish gives you the opportunity to remove dirt and lint with rubbing abrasives. Before you start to work, clean your working area thoroughly, and then let the dust settle for about 24 hours. Keep doors and windows closed. Don't work near heating/cooling registers or next to open windows, and never work outside. Wear lint-free clothes, and don't wear gloves.

Before you apply any finish, make sure you have all the materials you need. Set up your working space so that the piece of furniture will always be between you and the light; this makes it easy to see dust and lint on the newly finished surfaces. Work with clean tools and new finish materials, and make sure you have adequate light and ventilation. Clean all surfaces carefully with a tack cloth before applying the finish; if necessary, give the piece of furniture a final going-over with mineral spirits to remove dirt and fingerprints. Let the wood dry thoroughly before applying the finish. To keep the new finish smooth, remove specks of dust and lint from wet surfaces with an artists' brush or lint picker.

THE BASIC FINISHES

In most cases, how a piece of furniture stands up to wear is as important as how it looks, and durability is a primary consideration in choosing a finish. The most durable finishes, varnish and penetrating resin, are thus the two basic finishes for refinishing. Varnish is the more protective of the two because it is a surface coat; damage to the varnish does not always extend to the wood. Penetrating resin hardens in the wood itself; although it doesn't protect the surface from damage as effectively as varnish, it may stand up to heavy use better because it's easy to reapply and doesn't chip or craze.

Varnish

Varnish, one of the toughest of the finishes, is superior to the other traditional finishes; it enhances and gives warmth to the grain of the wood, and is resistant to impact, heat, abrasion, water, and alcohol. It can be used as a top coat over worn finishes. Varnish provides a clear finish, but it darkens the wood slightly; it is available in high-gloss, semigloss or satin, and matte or flat surface finishes. Varnish dries very slowly, and can be difficult to apply. Dust can be a problem.

Types of Varnish. The traditional varnish is based on natural resins and oils, and is thinned with mineral spirits or turpentine. Spar varnish is a natural varnish formulated to stay tacky; it should never be used for furniture. Synthetic varnishes are based on synthetic resins, and require special thinners. The best of the synthetic varnishes is the polyurethane type; polyurethanes are clear, non-yellowing, and very tough. Other synthetic varnishes are the phenolics, used for exterior and some marine work, and the alkyds, often used in colored preparations. Phenolic and alkyd varnishes yellow with age, and are not recommended for refinishing. With any type of varnish, look for quick drying to minimize dust problems. Use spray varnish only where brushing is impractical, such as on wicker or rattan.

Special Requirements. Natural varnish can be used with any stain or filler. The sealer for natural varnish is thinned shellac or a mixture of 1 part varnish and 1 part turpentine or mineral spirits. Do not mix brands or types of varnish. Polyurethane varnish is not compatible with all stains and fillers; before buying, read the labels to make sure you're using compatible materials. Some polyurethanes can be thinned for use as a sealer; some do not require sealers. Some sanding sealers are compatible with polyurethanes.

How to Apply Varnish. Apply varnish with a new, clean, natural-bristle brush. Use only new varnish; varnish that's been used several times may contain lumps of hardened varnish from around the sides and rim of the container. These lumps can really cause trouble. If you plan the job properly, you probably won't have enough varnish left to be wasteful. Leftover varnish can be used on parts that won't show, or projects where the finish isn't critical.

Bare wood to be finished with varnish must be properly prepared, sealed, and sanded. Finished wood to be top-coated must be cleaned and lightly sanded. Immediately before applying the varnish, clean each surface thoroughly with a tack cloth.

It's much easier to apply varnish to horizontal surfaces than vertical surfaces; before you start to work, turn the piece of furniture so that its major surfaces are horizontal. If the piece has drawers, doors, shelving,

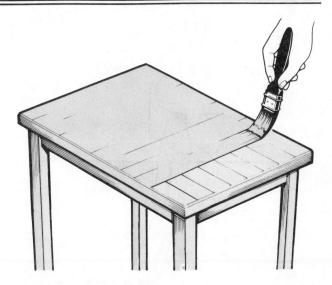

Apply varnish first along the grain of the wood, flowing it on in even strips. Then apply more varnish across the grain to level and even the surface.

and other removable parts, take them out or off and finish them horizontally. Work on only one surface at a time, and work on large surfaces last.

Apply varnish to the prepared wood with long, smooth, even strokes, laying the varnish on along the grain in strips the width of the brush. Do not touch the brush to the rim of the varnish container; shake or tap off excess varnish inside the container or on a strike can. The varnish should flow onto the surface of the wood, with no drag. If the brush starts to pull, or if you see small missed or thin spots, add about 1 ounce of thinner to the varnish—turpentine or mineral spirits for natural varnish; the thinner recommended by the manufacturer for polyurethane varnish. Stir the thinner gently into the varnish, being careful not to raise any bubbles.

After laying on an even coat of varnish in strips along the grain of the wood, apply more varnish in even strokes across the grain of the wood to level and even the surface. The varnish should be as even and level as possible, with no thick or thin spots, but a thin coat is better than a thick one—thick coats of varnish take longer to dry, and they tend to crack as the varnish ages. As you work, remove dust and lint from the wet finish with a rosin lint picker.

To finish each surface, tip off the wet varnish in the direction of the grain. Use an almost dry brush for this step. Holding the brush at a slight angle to the surface, very lightly stroke the surface of the varnish to remove brush marks and even the surface. Smooth the entire varnished surface, working in strips along the grain of the wood. As you work, pick off dust and lint with a lint picker. Any remaining brush marks will disappear as the varnish dries.

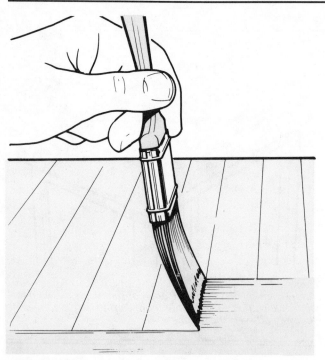

After leveling the varnish across the grain, smooth the surface by stroking it very lightly along the grain with an almost dry brush. Pick off dust and lint as you work.

Varnish must be applied carefully to prevent thick spots. At outside corners, work from the flat surface toward the corner; lift the brush as it nears the corner and before it flips down over the edge. This prevents a buildup of varnish along the edge. At inside corners, work an inch or two away from the corner; then brush the varnish into the corner, tip it off, and leave it alone. This method prevents buildup on many flat-surface brushings.

Spots that tend to hold varnish like tiny potholes should be coated just once with varnish and tipped just once with the brush. Repeated tipping will leave a bulge.

Brush lengthwise along rungs, spindles, and other turnings. On carved moldings, apply the finish to the carvings first with a fairly dry brush; then finish the flat surfaces with the tip of the brush. Finally, with a very dry brush, go over the carvings and then the flats, leveling the finish and removing any fat edges, sags, or runs. On raised panel doors, finish the panels first and then move on to the flat framing. The finish will build up at the miters in the frame where they meet the panel; remove the excess with a very dry brush, working from the corner out.

Drying and Recoating. Drying times for varnish average about 24 hours, but polyurethanes often dry more quickly. Dampness slows drying, so it's recommended that you extend all drying times, especially if you're applying varnish in humid or wet weather. Also, drying times are not necessarily *curing* times, and new varnish is easily damaged. Always let the finish dry at least 24 hours, or as long as the manufacturer recommends; if possible, let it dry a couple of days or more. Pick off lint and dust only while the surface is wet or sticky; too much interference could damage it.

Many varnishes require two or even three coats for a smooth finish—use your own judgment, and follow the manufacturer's recommendations. Between coats of varnish, let the first coat of varnish harden or dry, as recommended by the manufacturer. Some two-coat varnishes should be applied 10 to 15 hours from the time the first coat was applied, but in general, it's best to wait at least 24 hours—longer, if possible. When the first coat is completely dry, lightly sand the varnished wood in the direction of the grain, using grade 7/0 sandpaper on a padded sanding block. Abrade the

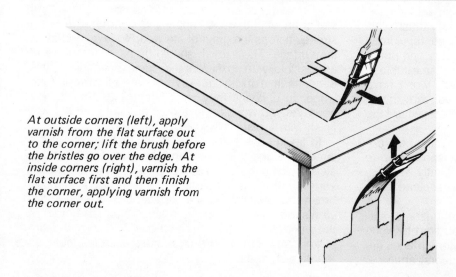

At outside corners (left), apply varnish from the flat surface out to the corner; lift the brush before the bristles go over the edge. At inside corners (right), varnish the flat surface first and then finish the corner, applying varnish from the corner out.

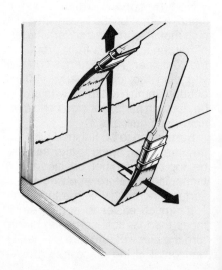

surface evenly, but don't cut it deeply. Clean away all sanding residue with a tack cloth and apply the second coat of varnish the same way as you did the first. Repeat this procedure, sanding the varnished wood carefully, if a third coat of varnish is required.

Penetrating Resin

Penetrating resin finishes, unlike varnish, are not surface finishes; they soak into the wood to harden the fibers themselves. Wood treated with penetrating resin has a very natural look and feel, as if it were unfinished; the grain is strongly highlighted. Penetrating resin is very durable, and withstands heavy wear; it is both easy to apply and easy to repair. It dries clear, but it darkens the wood slightly; it is also available in several stain colors. The finish may lack depth.

Because penetrating resin must soak into the wood, it is best used on open-grained woods; very close-grained woods may not absorb it deeply. On stripped wood, all old filler must be removed; if filler is left in the wood, the finish will not be absorbed. Penetrating resin is recommended for use on oily hardwoods, such as rosewood and teak, and is especially effective on oak and walnut. It is often preferable to varnish for use on large pieces of furniture and complex carvings. It dries relatively slowly, but because it is not a surface finish, dust is not a problem. A penetrating resin finish is very hard to remove for future refinishing.

Types of Penetrating Resin. Penetrating resin finishes are formulated with two different types of resins, phenolic and alkyd. There is little difference in performance between these types, but phenolic-base compounds may penetrate the wood more deeply than alkyd types.

Special Requirements. Penetrating resin can be used over any stain except varnish- or vinyl-base types. No filling or sealing is required. Before applying penetrating resin on bleached or stained surfaces, test it on a hidden part of the piece.

How to Apply Penetrating Resin. Wood to be finished with penetrating resin must be properly prepared and sanded. Because the finish does not coat the surface of the wood, any rough spots or other defects will be accentuated when the resin is applied. Immediately before applying the resin, clean the piece of furniture thoroughly with a tack cloth.

Whenever possible, penetrating resin should be applied to horizontal surfaces; if the piece of furniture has removable parts, remove them and finish them horizontally. Apply penetrating resin with a clean brush or cloth, or with No. 0000 steel wool; or pour it directly onto the wood. Work on small areas at a time. On rungs or spindles, apply the resin with a clean cloth, one rung at a time.

Spread the resin liberally and evenly over the wood. The appearance of the surface isn't critical, but the amount of resin used on each surface should be consistent. As you work, watch the wood surface. Some open-grained woods soak up the finish very quickly; others—especially close-grained hardwoods—absorb it slowly, and may not absorb much. Apply resin until the wood stops absorbing it.

Let the resin set for about 30 to 45 minutes. During this time, keep the surface wet, adding more resin to any dry spots that appear. All surfaces should be shiny. After 30 to 45 minutes, when the wood will not absorb any more resin and the surface is still wet, firmly wipe off the excess finish with clean, absorbent cloths. The surface of the wood should be completely dry, with no wet, shiny spots.

Drying and Recoating. Let the newly applied resin dry for 24 hours. If glossy patches appear on the wood during the drying period, remove them immediately; add resin to these areas to soften the dried finish, and wipe off the liquid resin so that the wood is dry.

After 24 hours, smooth the wood gently with No. 000 or 0000 steel wool; then clean it thoroughly with a tack cloth. Apply a second coat of penetrating resin, letting it penetrate and wiping off the excess as above. If necessary on very open-grained woods, apply a third coat of resin; wait 24 hours and smooth the surface with steel wool before application, as above. No wax or other surface coat is needed.

THE CLASSIC FINISHES

Varnish, first natural and then synthetic, has long been the choice for a durable finish. The other traditional finishes—shellac, lacquer, wax, and oil—are neither as tough nor as durable as varnish. But because each has its own distinctive advantages and characteristics, the classic finishes are still used today.

Shellac, the least durable of all finishes, is also the easiest to apply, and it dries very quickly. Used with linseed oil, it's the basis of the traditional French polish finish. The drawback is that shellac is very easily damaged by water or alcohol. Lacquer is similar, but tougher; it dries even faster than shellac, and is very hard to apply evenly. Today lacquer is used chiefly by manufacturers, or, for small jobs, in spray cans.

The other two traditional finishes are used less frequently. Wax, sometimes used on very hard woods, is not really a permanent finish, but it's easy to apply and maintain. Modern sealer stain systems use wax as a protective top coat. Oil, the original wood sealer, is still used where a rich natural finish is desired. The traditional oil is linseed oil, which is very hard to apply and maintain properly. Modern finishing oils, both natural and synthetic, are much easier to use.

Although these finishes are not recommended for most refinishing jobs, they can be very effective where durability is not important or where you want to achieve a particular character. Experiment with the classics on small pieces before you use them on large or valuable furniture; if you don't like your results, stick to the basic finishes.

Shellac

Shellac is the easiest of the classic finishes to apply. It produces a very fine, mellow finish, and accentuates the natural grain of the wood; it is especially attractive on walnut, mahogany, and fine veneer woods. It polishes well, and is the basis for the traditional French polish finish on very fine furniture. Shellac is applied in several thin coats. It dries fast, and can be recoated after four hours; it is commonly used as a sealer under other finishes. Application mistakes are easy to fix.

The big drawback to shellac is that it is not durable. Shellac is easily damaged, and dissolves in both water and alcohol; white rings are usually a problem. Shellac cannot be applied in very humid weather, because humidity turns it white; shellac finishes absorb moisture, and sometimes turn hazy or white with age. Repairs are easy, but frequent retouching is necessary. Shellac tends to be soft after it dries, so waxing is almost essential to protect the surface. It is best used on decorative pieces that don't have to stand up to hard wear.

Shellac Colors and Cuts. Shellac is available in two colors, white and orange. White shellac is used for light woods, and is thinned with denatured alcohol for use as a sealer. It can be tinted with alcohol-soluble aniline dye, and is sometimes available in colors. Orange shellac gives an amber color to the wood; this is often desirable on dark woods. It is especially attractive on walnut, mahogany, and teak.

Shellac is sold in several cuts, or concentrations; the most common type is a 4-pound cut. Shellac usually must be thinned or cut with denatured alcohol before application, as directed by the manufacturer. For sealer, thin 1 part of 3- or 4-pound-cut white shellac with 4 parts denatured alcohol; for finish coats, thin 1

part 4-pound shellac with 2 parts alcohol. The chart below lists thinning proportions for the common cuts of shellac.

Special Requirements. Shellac can be used over any stain except alcohol-base types (NGR), and over any filler. Thinned shellac is recommended for sealer coats. Use denatured alcohol to thin shellac; use alcohol or ammonia for cleanup. Shellac has a very short shelf life; old shellac does not dry properly. Buy just enough for the job, and junk any leftover shellac. Some manufacturers shelf-date shellac.

How to Apply Shellac. Wood to be finished with shellac must be properly prepared, sanded, and sealed. Immediately before applying shellac, clean each surface thoroughly with a tack cloth. Use a new, clean, good-quality brush, and use only new shellac, thinned to a 1-pound cut. Work on one area at a time.

To apply shellac, flow it liberally onto the surface, working in long, smooth strokes along the grain of the wood. Keep the surface really wet with the shellac, and apply the finish from dry to wet edges. After coating the surface completely, tip off the shellac along the grain of the wood. Use an almost dry brush for this step. Holding the brush at a slight angle to the surface, very lightly stroke the surface of the shellac to remove brush marks and even the surface. Smooth the entire shellacked surface, working in strips along the grain of the wood.

Drying and Recoating. Shellac dries in about 30 minutes, and can be recoated after four hours. Let the new shellac set for a full four hours. Make sure drying time is adequate—because shellac is soft, it can pick up sandpaper grains or steel wool shreds if it isn't completely dry. This can result in a nightmare of smoothing to remove the debris.

When the shellac is completely dry, lightly sand the surface with grade 7/0 open-coat sandpaper on a padded sanding block. Clean the sanded surface thoroughly with a tack cloth and then apply a second coat of shellac, as above. Let the shellac dry for four hours;

Shellac Thinning Proportions

| Cut | 3-pound base | | 4-pound base | | 5-pound base | |
	Shellac	Alcohol	Shellac	Alcohol	Shellac	Alcohol
½-pound	1 part	4 parts	1 part	5 parts	1 part	7 parts
1-pound	3 parts	4 parts	1 part	2 parts	1 part	2 parts
2-pound	5 parts	2 parts	4 parts	3 parts	1 part	1 part
2½-pound	5 parts	1 part	2 parts	1 part	3 parts	2 parts
3-pound	—	—	4 parts	1 part	2 parts	1 part

then repeat, sanding and cleaning the surface, to apply a third coat. Additional coats of shellac can be added, if you want a smoother surface; let each coat dry thoroughly before applying a new one, and buff the finish with fine steel wool between coats.

Let the final coat of shellac harden for 48 hours. With grade No. 0000 steel wool, remove the gloss from the finished surface, rubbing carefully along the grain of the wood. Do *not* rub across the grain. When the gloss is completely removed, let the piece of furniture stand for 48 hours. Then apply a good-quality paste wax to the finished wood, and buff the surface to a shine with a soft cloth or the buffing attachment of an electric drill.

The French Polish Finish. This shellac finishing technique produces a much more durable surface than the standard shellac finish. French-polished surfaces have a very distinctive, velvety sheen, and the grain and color of the wood are emphasized. It is best used on close-grained woods and fine veneers. Use only water stain or spirit-based NGR stain under French polish; other types may bleed or lift.

To apply a French polish finish, mix 2 tablespoons of boiled linseed oil into 1 pint of 1-pound-cut shellac. Make a palm-size pad of cheesecloth, and wrap it in a clean, lint-free linen or cotton cloth. The pad should just fit in your palm. Dip the pad into the shellac/oil mixture; don't soak it. Make sure the surface of the pad is not wrinkled.

Apply the shellac/oil mixture to the prepared wood, spreading it evenly along the grain to cover the entire surface; work with a quick padding stroke, blending your strokes carefully. Then rub the wet surface with the pad, using a firm circular or figure-eight motion over the wood. Continue this circular rubbing for about 45 minutes, using plenty of downward pressure and adding shellac as the mixture is worked into the wood. The surface should be evenly glossy, with no dark spots or stroke marks.

Let the rubbed shellac/oil mixture dry for 24 hours; then apply another coat of shellac/oil as above. Rub the second coat in for 45 minutes, and let it dry for two to three days; then apply a third coat the same way.

Let the wood dry for at least a week, but not more than 10 days, after the final coat. Finally, clean the surface, wax the finished wood with a good-quality paste wax, and buff it to a fine sheen.

Lacquer

Lacquer is the fastest-drying of the finishes, more durable than shellac; it is very thin, and must be applied in many thin coats. It is available in high-gloss, satin, and matte finishes, in clear form and in several clear stain colors. Dust-free drying is not a problem, but because lacquer dries so fast—sometimes almost instantly—it is very difficult to work with. Brushing lacquers are not recommended for amateur use; spraying lacquers

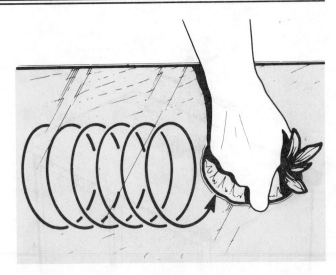

The French polish finish is achieved by hand-rubbing. Apply the shellac/oil mixture and rub it in with a circular or figure-eight motion; continue rubbing for 45 minutes, adding more finish as necessary.

must be applied with a motorized spray gun. Application is tricky, and lacquer fumes are both toxic and explosive. For these reasons, lacquer is not usually used in amateur refinishing. For small jobs, lacquer can be applied with aerosol spray cans. This is expensive, but it works well.

Special Requirements. Lacquer can be used on most woods, but it cannot be used on mahogany and rosewood; the oils in these woods will bleed through the finish. Lacquer can be used over lacquer-base, NGR, and water stains, and over lacquer-base fillers. It cannot be used over other finishes, or over oil-base stains or many fillers; the solvents in lacquer will dissolve other finishes and incompatible stains and fillers. Thinned lacquer or shellac or a compatible lacquer-base sanding sealer should be used as a sealer under a lacquer finish.

How to Apply Lacquer. Wood to be finished with lacquer must be properly prepared, sanded, and sealed. Immediately before applying lacquer, clean the piece of furniture thoroughly with a tack cloth. Use only aerosol spray lacquer, and protect your working area with dropcloths or newspaper. Make sure ventilation is adequate.

Before applying lacquer, test the spray can on a piece of newspaper or cardboard. Spray cans have different patterns of spray; practicing and watching the test spray pattern will give you enough control to properly cover the surface you're finishing.

Apply lacquer slowly and evenly, holding the spray can upright about 18 inches away from the surface of the wood. If you work farther away than this, the lac-

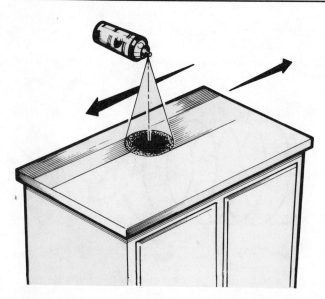

With the can about 18 inches from the surface, spray lacquer in even strips from side to side, top to bottom. Overlap the strips slightly to equalize the thickness of the lacquer film.

quer will tend to "orange peel," dimpling like the skin on an orange. If you work closer than 18 inches, too much lacquer may be applied to the surface, causing runs and sags in the finish. First spray the top edge of the surface; then cover the entire surface in horizontal strips, from side to side, top to bottom. As you work, overlap the lacquer spray patterns slightly. The edges of each sprayed area are thin; the centers are thick. Overlapping equalizes the thickness of the lacquer film, keeping the surface even. Never try to equalize the film by brushing the lacquer. Apply only a thin coat of lacquer; this finish must be applied in many thin layers.

Drying and Recoating. Lacquer dries in no more than half an hour, but it must cure completely between coats. Let the newly sprayed wood dry for about 48 hours, or as directed by the manufacturer. Then lightly smooth the surface with No. 000 steel wool, and clean it thoroughly with a tack cloth. Apply a second coat of lacquer as above. For a smoother finish, let the second coat dry for 48 hours, smooth the surface with No. 000 steel wool, and apply a third coat of lacquer as above.

Runs and sags are usually caused by too much lacquer, but they don't always appear on the first couple of coats. The solvent in each coat of lacquer softens the dried lacquer under it to meld the coats together. As you apply more coats of lacquer, the bottom coats soften, and the lacquer film gets thicker; any unevenness can cause sags. For a very rich, deep finish, use many very thin coats of lacquer. Let the lacquer dry completely between coats, and rub the surface between coats with grade FFF powdered pumice and

boiled linseed oil on a cheesecloth or felt pad.

After applying the final coat of lacquer, let the piece of furniture dry for 48 hours; then lightly buff the lacquered surface with No. 0000 steel wool. Clean the surface thoroughly with a tack cloth and apply a good-quality paste wax. Buff the waxed surface to a fine gloss.

Waxes and Sealer Stains

Paste wax, often used to protect finishes, is sometimes used to finish bare wood. This is most successful on hard, close-grained woods, such as maple, that have been sanded absolutely smooth. Some waxes have color added, for use on dark woods such as walnut. These waxes add color to the wood, and are especially helpful if the finish on the wood is blotchy, but they do not stain the wood or restore the finish. Paste wax is easy to apply, and is nonsticky and heat-resistant, but it is easily damaged and liable to wear. It must be reapplied periodically. Paste wax is more commonly used over a sealer stain to color, seal, and finish new or stripped wood.

Sealer stain finishes, such as the commercial Minwax system, are available in several colors. Sealer stains produce a very even color, with no lap marks or dark spots. They are fairly tough, and are very easy to apply; they are not very water-resistant, and must often be recoated periodically.

Special Requirements. Paste wax can be applied directly over prepared bare or stained wood; thinned shellac is recommended as a sealer coat. Sealer stains should be applied directly over prepared bare wood; no other sealer is required. Open-grained woods should be filled before a wax finish is applied; any paste filler is compatible. Wax and sealer stain finishes can be used on new or stripped wood.

How to Apply Paste Wax. Wood to be finished with paste wax must be thoroughly sanded and sealed with a coat of thinned shellac. When the sealer is completely dry, rub the wood along the grain with No. 0000 steel wool; then clean the piece of furniture thoroughly with a tack cloth.

Apply paste wax sparingly with a clean, lint-free cloth pad, rubbing the wax on with a circular motion to form a thin, even coating. Work on a small area at a time. Some manufacturers recommend that the wax be applied with a damp—not wet—pad. If you use water, make sure the surface is dry before you polish it.

Let the wax dry completely, as recommended by the manufacturer. Then wipe the waxed surface firmly with a clean cloth to remove excess wax. When the waxed surface is even, polish it to a shine with a clean cloth. To complete the finish, apply one or two more coats of wax, as above. Polish each coat completely before applying the next coat.

How to Apply a Sealer Stain Finish. Wood to be finished with a sealer stain finish, such as Minwax, must be properly prepared and sanded; no other preparation is necessary. Thoroughly mix the sealer stain. Apply the stain evenly along the grain with a clean brush or cloth, and let it stand for 10 to 15 minutes; then wipe off the excess with a clean cloth. Let the wood dry for 24 hours and apply a second coat of stain, as above. To complete the finish, apply one or two coats of paste wax, as above. Polish each coat thoroughly with a clean cloth.

Oils

Hand-rubbed oil finishes can be beautiful, but only if they're properly applied. Oil is penetrating and durable; it is water- and alcohol-resistant, and gives the wood an attractive natural sheen and texture. Danish and tung oil finishes are far superior to the traditional linseed oil; linseed oil is sticky and hard to apply. Any oil finish must be reapplied periodically, but Danish and tung oil require far less reapplication than linseed oil.

Types of Oil Finishes. Modern oil finishes—Danish oil, a synthetic, and natural tung-oil sealers—are penetrating finishes, but they should be applied periodically. Tung-oil finishes are available in semigloss and high-gloss forms, and also in several stain colors. Danish oil usually has a satin finish.

A linseed oil finish is rich and glossy, but many applications are required for a good finish. The classic linseed oil finish is a mixture of equal parts of boiled linseed oil and turpentine. There are many variations on the linseed oil finish. One of the best of them is the Mary Roalman finish, which consists of equal parts of boiled linseed oil, turpentine, and natural varnish. Mix the linseed oil finishes several days before you use them. For most pieces, a pint of each ingredient is plenty.

Special Requirements. Oil finishes can be applied directly over prepared bare or stained wood. Only water or NGR stains should be used; oil-base stains interfere with the penetration of the oil. Stain-color tung-oil sealers stain and finish in one operation. Very open-grained woods should be filled before an oil finish is applied; any paste filler is compatible. No sealing is required.

How to Apply an Oil Finish. Wood to be finished with oil must be thoroughly sanded, filled, and smoothed; no sealing is necessary. Before applying the finish, clean the piece of furniture thoroughly with a tack cloth.

Apply the oil—Danish oil, tung oil sealer, linseed oil, or the Mary Roalman mixture—with a clean cheesecloth pad, using a circular or figure-eight motion to work it into the wood. Apply oil evenly and liberally, until the

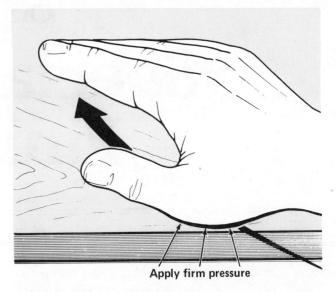

Apply firm pressure

Apply oil liberally until the wood stops absorbing it; working along the grain, rub it firmly into the wood with the heels of your hands. Then wipe off all excess oil.

wood has stopped absorbing it; work on one surface at a time. Apply oil until the wood is evenly oiled and the surface has stopped absorbing.

Rub the oil firmly into the wood with the heels of your hands, working along the grain. Continue rubbing for about 15 minutes; as you rub, the warmth you generate will help the oil penetrate into the wood. Danish oil and tung oil may not require such extensive rubbing; follow the manufacturer's specific instructions. Finally, after thoroughly rubbing all surfaces, wipe the piece of furniture clean with a clean cloth. You must remove all excess oil; there should be no oil—or, if you're using a linseed finish, only a very thin film of oil—on the surface of the wood.

Drying and Recoating. Danish oil and tung oil dry more quickly than linseed oil. In most cases, they can be reapplied after 12 to 24 hours; follow the manufacturer's specific instructions. Linseed-oil finishes must dry for about a week; drying takes longer in very humid weather. Do not recoat a linseed-oil finish until it's completely dry, with no trace of stickiness.

When the first coat of oil is completely dry, apply further coats until the finish is rich and hard. Danish oil and tung-oil sealers may require only one additional application, but linseed-oil finishes should be given 10 to 20 additional coats. Rub each additional coat of oil thoroughly into the wood, as above, and then wipe off all excess oil. Let each coat of oil dry thoroughly before applying the next—at least one week between the first several coats, longer between later coats. If the oil isn't completely dry between coats, the finished surface will be sticky.

Chapter 7
Special-Effect Finishes

When you're aiming for a special look, or want an accent piece or a particular decorative effect, there's more to refinishing than the basic finish. With a few special-effect finishing techniques, you can decorate newly finished furniture, refurbish an old piece without stripping it, or add distinction to an inexpensive unfinished piece. Any finish can be dressed up with these techniques—use your imagination to create any effect you like.

Whatever finish you're working on, it must be clean and smooth; if you're covering it completely, it must be properly prepared. For special effects done with paint or varnish, make sure the materials you use are compatible with the finish on the piece. This is especially important with lacquer finishes.

ENAMELING

Unlike clear finishes, enamel can be used over an old finish. It is tough, attractive, and easy to take care of. It covers a lot of flaws—poor-quality or uninteresting wood, badly stained surfaces, and pieces made with very different types of wood can all be rescued with a coat of bright enamel. Used over bare wood or over an old finish, enamel can create a striking accent piece. Used under a glaze, it is the most common base for antiquing.

Types of Enamel. Where furniture is concerned, enamel should never be confused with paint. Paint consists of pigments in an application vehicle or medium; good enamel consists of pigments in a varnish, lacquer, or oil base. While enamel is as tough as varnish, paint produces a soft finish, and is not recommended for use on furniture. Oil-based enamel is generally superior to the latex type.

Enamel is available in high-gloss, semigloss, and flat or matte forms. If you're enameling a piece of furniture as an accent for a room, you may want a shiny finish, but most fine enameled furniture has a satin finish, not high-gloss. In general, serious furniture should probably be satin-finished; just-for-fun pieces are usually shiny. Buy enamel in stock colors, or have it mixed at the paint store.

Special Requirements. On bare wood, enamel can be used with any filler. Finished surfaces to be enameled must be sealed with thinned shellac; before enamel is applied, all surfaces should be undercoated. Shiny enamel emphasizes flaws, so surfaces to be covered with this type must be very smooth. Enamel cannot be used over wax.

Enameling Over an Old Finish. Unless a piece of furniture has intricate carvings already clogged by the old finish, stripping is not required before enamel is applied. To prepare a finished piece for enameling, sand it to remove any obvious flaws and chip marks. The surface must be smooth, but it isn't necessary to remove the old finish completely. Clean the sanded wood thoroughly with a tack cloth, and apply a sealer coat of thinned shellac; let it dry completely, sand the piece lightly with grade 7/0 sandpaper, and remove the sanding debris with a tack cloth. To prepare a stripped or unfinished piece, sand and seal the wood as for any finish application, and clean it with a tack cloth.

How to Apply an Enamel Finish. Wood to be finished with enamel must be properly sanded, filled, and sealed; finished surfaces must be sanded and sealed. Before applying enamel, clean the piece of furniture thoroughly with a tack cloth.

Before applying the enamel, you must undercoat the piece of furniture; commercial enamel undercoater is available. This undercoater is usually white; use it white or have it tinted to match the enamel. The undercoat should never be darker than the enamel.

Apply the undercoat with a clean, good-quality brush; make sure the undercoat is thoroughly mixed. Brush the undercoat smoothly and evenly along the grain of the wood, flowing it on to cover the surface completely. Carefully smooth the surface to even out any thick spots. Brush marks will almost disappear as the undercoat dries.

Let the undercoat dry for at least three days, or as directed by the manufacturer; then lightly sand the undercoated surfaces with grade 7/0 sandpaper. Remove all sanding debris with a tack cloth.

When the undercoat is complete, apply the enamel. Use a clean, good-quality brush, of the type specified by the enamel manufacturer; mix the enamel thoroughly but gently. Apply the enamel with long, smooth, even strokes, laying it on along the grain or length of the wood in strips the width of the brush. Use enough enamel to flow smoothly onto the surface, but not so much that you leave thick spots.

After laying on an even coat of enamel in strips, apply more enamel across the grain or width of the wood to level and even the surface. The enamel should be as even as possible, with no thick or thin spots, but as with varnish, a thin coat is better than a thick one. Thick coats of enamel dry extremely slowly, and tend to stay soft for a long time.

To finish each surface, tip off the enamel along the grain or length of the wood, using an almost dry brush. Holding the brush at a slight angle to the surface, very lightly stroke the surface of the enamel to remove brush marks and even the surface. Smooth the entire enameled surface, working in strips along the grain or length of the wood. As you work, pick off dust and lint with a lint picker. Brush marks will disappear as the enamel dries.

On vertical surfaces, enamel is likely to sag or run. Work with a fairly dry brush, applying enamel from dry to wet surfaces. As you finish each surface, carefully inspect it for runs and sags. With the brush in a tipped position, and moving the brush as you come onto the surface with the bristles, tip the finish. Keep the stroke in motion as you come through the sag or run and as the tip of the brush leaves the surface. By keeping the brush in motion before, during, and following the tipping, you will avoid brush marks. Watch the enamel carefully as it dries; sags and runs are especially liable to occur after the enamel has set for 10 to 15 minutes. Tip off sags and runs immediately when you spot them.

Enamel must be applied carefully to prevent thick spots. At outside corners, work from the flat surface toward the corner; lift the brush as it nears the corner and before it flips down over the edge. This prevents a buildup of enamel along the edge. At inside corners, work an inch or two away from the corner; then brush the enamel into the corner, tip it off, and leave it alone. This method prevents buildup on many flat-surface brushings. Spots that tend to hold enamel like tiny potholes should be coated just once with enamel and tipped just once with the brush. Repeated tipping will leave a bulge.

Brush lengthwise along rungs, spindles, and other turnings. On carved moldings, apply the finish to the carvings first with a fairly dry brush; then finish the flat surfaces with the tip of the brush. Finally, with a very dry brush, go over the carvings and then the flats,

leveling the finish and removing any fat edges, sags, or runs. On raised panel doors, finish the panels first and then move onto the flat framing. The finish will build up at the miters in the frame where they meet the panel; remove the excess with a very dry brush, working from the corner out.

Drying and Recoating. Let the enamel dry for several days, or as directed by the manufacturer. Then lightly sand the surface with grade 7/0 sandpaper and a padded sanding block, and clean the piece of furniture thoroughly with a tack cloth. Apply a second coat of enamel, as above, and let it dry completely.

Enamel can be finished in several ways. For a tough, shiny surface, apply a third coat of enamel, as above; sand the second coat lightly before applying more enamel. Or let the piece of furniture dry for at least a month, and then apply a coat of paste wax and buff it to a shine.

ANTIQUING

Antiquing is the technique of glazing a base finish to simulate age or create an interesting color effect. Enamel is the most common base for antiquing, but varnished, shellacked, and lacquered surfaces can also be glazed. Antiquing is not recommended for real antiques, but it can work wonders with a thrift-store find or a cheap unfinished piece.

Antiquing Materials. Antiquing kits, sold in paint and hardware stores, include both base enamel and a coordinated or contrasting glaze; many colors and combinations are available. Any sound flat or gloss enamel, varnish, shellac, or lacquer finish can be treated with glaze; look for transparent antiquing glaze, in muted tones of umber and burnt sienna or in white, gold, black, or colors. The greater the contrast between base and glaze, and the brighter the glaze color, the more obvious it will be that the piece of furniture is antiqued. If you're working over an existing finish, make sure the glaze is compatible.

The Base Coat. A piece of furniture to be antique-finished must be clean and in good repair. Remove all hardware. If you're antiquing an unfinished piece of furniture or covering an old finish, sand and seal the wood, as detailed above for enameling. On finished pieces to be covered completely, clean the wood thoroughly and then treat it with sanding deglosser to dull the surface; if there are still any shiny spots, buff them with No. 0000 steel wool. Sand out any chips in the old finish so that the surface is smooth. On pieces to be glazed over an existing finish, clean the wood thoroughly with a detergent solution and dry it well; then wipe it with denatured alcohol. Let the prepared wood dry for 24 hours.

If you're working on an unfinished piece or covering

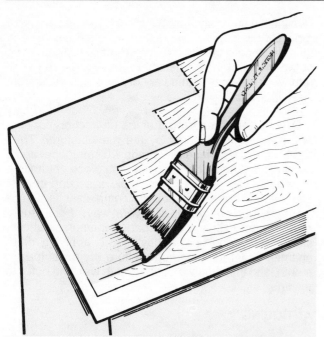

Antiquing consists of a glaze applied over a base finish; the first step is applying an enamel base coat to the wood.

The Glaze. When the base coat is completely dry, or the existing base finish is prepared, apply the antiquing glaze. Use a contrasting color for an obvious antiqued look, a muted umber or burnt sienna to simulate age. Apply the glaze with a clean brush.

Antiquing glaze sets quickly, and the surfaces you glaze first will retain more color than the ones you glaze later. Working on one surface at a time, apply glaze to moldings, carvings, and decorated areas, and then to flat areas. On large surfaces, the glaze can be applied in several stages, if necessary.

Let the glaze dry until it starts to dull, as directed by the manufacturer. Then carefully wipe the glaze off with a soft cloth, flat surfaces first, so that the base coat retains color only at areas to be highlighted. Work from the center of each surface out to the edges, wiping carefully along the grain of the wood. Remove the glaze completely from high spots; leave some of it in low spots, in corners, in carvings or decorations, and along edges and moldings. The surfaces wiped last will retain the most glaze; leave the parts you want to highlight until last.

Let the glazed surface dry completely, as directed by the manufacturer.

Textured Glazes. For a bolder look, you can get different design effects by texturing the glaze with different materials, and leaving more glaze on. Before using these texturing methods on a piece of furniture, experiment on a piece of scrap wood given an enamel base coat.

Texturing the glaze can be done with almost anything—cheesecloth, crumpled newspaper, plastic

an old finish, apply a base finish coat of flat or gloss enamel; use the application techniques detailed above for enameling. Let the enamel dry completely. If necessary, apply a second base coat; sand the surface lightly, clean it, and apply the enamel. Let the final coat of enamel dry completely, at least two days.

When the enamel base is dry, brush the glaze on over it, one surface at a time. For glaze retention on highlights, cover highlight areas first, then flat surfaces.

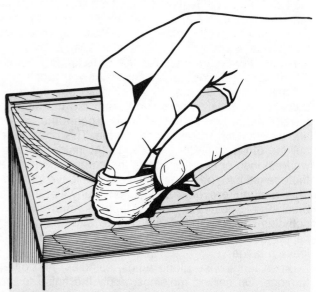

Let the glaze dry until it starts to dull; then wipe it off. Work from the center out, leaving glaze in low spots, in carvings, and along the edges.

wrap, a sponge, or whatever you have on hand. Remove a little glaze or almost all of it, whichever you prefer. For a wood-grain texture, use a cheesecloth pad; wipe the glaze off in long, even strokes, and then dab it with a scrap piece of carpeting or a stiff-bristled brush. Crumpled newspaper or plastic wrap produces a marble effect; a dry sponge makes a random stipple. Use a burlap bag or a towel for a scratched look. For a leather texture, let the glaze get almost dry; then pad it with a piece of fiberglass insulation.

Protecting the Surface. Antiqued finishes can be left uncoated, but for a more durable surface, seal the piece of furniture with semigloss or high-gloss varnish. Make sure the varnish is compatible with the antiqued finish. Apply the varnish directly over the antiquing, as detailed in Chapter 6 for varnish finishes.

FLYSPECKING

Flyspecking is the random spattering of furniture with tiny drops of paint; the effect is of aged and worn wood. Some very expensive furniture is flyspecked, but this technique can be especially effective in finishing inexpensive pieces. Flyspecking isn't really deceptive, but it can be attractive.

Flyspecking Materials. Any thin flat black paint can be used for flyspecking. For colored specks, use thinned shellac tinted with aniline dye; orange or brown is effective on medium-brown wood. Thin the paint or shellac so that it spatters in fine droplets; make sure it's compatible with the finish.

How to Apply Flyspecking. A piece of furniture to be flyspecked must be clean; if you're finishing the piece, add flyspecking after sealing but before the finish is applied. Before working on a piece of furniture, practice the specking technique on a piece of cardboard or scrap wood.

The easiest way to apply the specks is by spattering the thinned paint or shellac through a piece of wire screening. Dip a toothbrush into the paint or shellac and flick the bristles with your thumb; work just far enough from the surface to produce a fine, even spatter. Experiment to find the best brushing angle; practice until you can cover the test surface evenly, and then apply the specks to the piece of furniture.

Flyspecking can be used over an entire surface or to accentuate edges and corners. Apply the specks in any density desired, working evenly over the surface. Use only tiny spatters of paint or shellac; to speck an area more heavily, use repeated spatters. Let the flyspecked piece dry completely.

Protecting the Surface. Flyspecked surfaces should be sealed with varnish. Apply the varnish directly over the flyspecking, as detailed in Chapter 6.

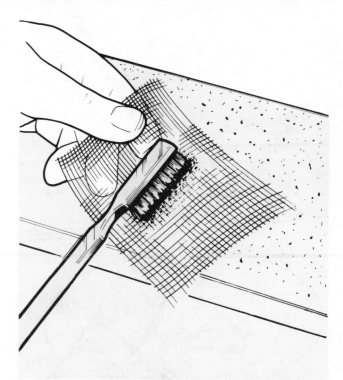

To flyspeck a surface, carefully spatter thinned paint or shellac with a toothbrush, through a piece of wire screening.

GILDING

Ornate carvings or turnings and carved mirror and picture frames can be finished with gold to create a special look. The traditional gilding method is gold-leafing, done with thin sheets of gold foil. Gold leaf is beautiful and durable, but it's also very expensive, and isn't used much in furniture work. Bronzing, a more recent technique, is done with powdered gold, either mixed into a vehicle or applied directly; it may fade with time. Bronze powder is made in gold, silver, bronze, copper, and colors; it is often used for stencils on furniture.

The easiest way to apply gold or other metals is wax gilding. Wax gilt is a paste, made in gold, silver, bronze, copper, and colors and sold at craft and art supply stores. It's inexpensive and looks very much like gold leaf. For moldings, small-area highlighting, and striping, wax gilt is the best choice. Use it over gold leaf paint for the best results.

How to Apply Wax Gilt. A surface to be gilded must be clean; remove all wax and dirt. If you're working on a picture frame, clean the surface very gently with a damp cloth, and let it dry thoroughly.

For the deepest gold effect, paint the area to be gilded with liquid gold leaf paint, using a ½-inch brush. Let the paint dry completely, about 30 minutes, and then apply the wax gilt.

Apply wax gilt sparingly, smoothing it back and forth to bring out the sheen. When the gilt has set, buff it lightly.

Spray paint onto the stencil in short, even bursts. To prevent spattering, mask the piece of furniture with paper.

To apply the gilt, dip an artists' brush or a piece of soft cloth into turpentine and then into the gilt; if the gilt is in a tube, squeeze a little out so it's easier to work with. Wax gilt is thick; apply it sparingly, smoothing it on. Press gently as you work, smoothing or brushing back and forth, to bring out the sheen of the gold. When the entire surface is covered, let the gilt set for about an hour; then carefully buff the surface, in one direction only, with a soft cloth. The buffing distributes and highlights the gilt. No surface protection or further finishing is necessary.

STENCILS

Whether you want art deco or Pennsylvania Dutch, a drawing or a child's name, stencils are a quick and almost foolproof way of getting it. Stencils can be applied over any finish; they are easiest to work with when used over varnish that's still slightly tacky. When the surface to be decorated is completely dry, the stencil must be very carefully attached so that the edges of the design don't blur. Use paint for informal designs, bronze powder—gold, silver, bronze, copper, or colors—for a more formal effect.

Cutting the Stencil. Use stencil paper or architects' linen, available at art supply stores, to make the stencil; if your design has more than one color, make a separate stencil for each color. For large or complex designs, make several small stencils instead of one large one. Trace your design carefully onto the stencil paper or architects' linen, and cut it out with a sharp craft knife. Make sure all corners and curves are sharp and accurate.

How to Apply a Painted Stencil. Brushing paint over a stencil is tricky, and requires a special brush. For the best results, use high-gloss or semigloss spray paint or enamel. Make sure the stencil paint is compatible with the finish.

Surfaces to be stenciled must be clean; remove all wax and dirt. If you're decorating a newly varnished piece of furniture, work while the varnish is still tacky. Carefully press the stencil into place on the tacky surface, smoothing it down flat on the wood. Make sure all cut edges adhere to the varnish, but be careful not to touch the varnish or you'll leave fingerprints. On dry surfaces, attach the stencil carefully with masking tape. If the finish is new, make sure it's completely set; otherwise the tape may damage it. Mask the entire piece of furniture with newspaper.

Spray paint onto the stencil in short, even applications; cover the stencil surface completely, but don't let the paint get thick enough to sag or drip. Let the paint dry almost completely; then remove the stencil. Repeat the process for each color of the design; make sure each color is completely dry before applying the next color.

How to Apply a Bronze Powder Stencil. Surfaces to be stenciled must be clean; remove all wax and dirt. Bronze powder must be applied over varnish. If you're working on a newly varnished piece of furniture, apply the stencil while the varnish is still slightly tacky. If you're working on an old or completely dry finish, apply a thin coat of varnish over the surface to be stenciled, and let it dry until it's just tacky—about 30 minutes to two hours. Make sure the varnish is compatible with the existing finish.

Carefully press the stencil into place on the varnished surface, smoothing it down flat. Make sure all cut edges adhere to the varnish, but be careful not to touch the varnish or you'll leave fingerprints. Masking the piece of furniture is not necessary.

Apply the bronze powder with a piece of velvet or soft flannel over your index finger, or make a small pad out of the fabric. Working with only a little powder, dip the velvet into the bronze powder and smudge it into the exposed areas of the stencil. Bronze powder can be applied evenly, but you can give your designs depth by shading it and rounding your strokes. Work from the edges in to bronze each area of the stencil.

Repeat the process for each color of the design. If you must overlap stencils to apply the colors, let the varnish dry completely between colors. Remove excess bronze powder with warm water and a soft brush; blot the wood dry and let it air-dry for about an hour. Apply another thin coat of varnish to the unfinished area, let it get tacky, and repeat the stenciling process. When the design is complete, let it dry and then remove excess bronze powder as above.

Protecting the Surface. To prevent damage to paint or bronze powder, stenciled surfaces should be sealed with varnish. Apply the varnish directly over the stencils, as detailed in Chapter 6.

STRIPING

On enameled or antiqued furniture, edge stripes can add distinction to flat surfaces—use one thin border stripe or paint multiple stripes or geometric borders. Tabletops, chair seats, and similar areas are good candidates for striping, but any flat surface can be decorated with stripes. Use high-gloss or semigloss enamel, slightly thinned; make sure it's compatible with the existing finish.

Freehand Striping. Freehand stripes take a steady hand and a good brush, but they aren't difficult on a fairly small piece. The surface to be striped must be clean; remove all wax and dirt. Use a good-quality artists' brush, with a small diameter and a good point. Practice striping on a piece of cardboard before you work on a piece of furniture.

Stripes close to the edge of a surface can be applied without a straightedge or other guide. Hold the brush

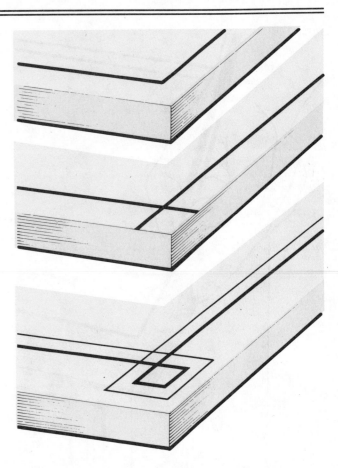

Edge stripes can add distinction to flat surfaces; use a single or multiple stripe, crossed lines, or a simple geometric.

with your thumb and first two fingers and rest your other two fingers on the edge of the surface; keeping the brush steady on the surface, draw your hand along the edge. This method is effective for edge stripes on curved or straight surfaces. For stripes too far from a straight edge for this technique, use a yardstick as a guide to draw your hand along; have an assistant hold the stick in place as you paint.

Apply enamel carefully, loading the brush enough to make a complete stripe but not enough to blob or drip. Keep your pressure steady as you draw the brush along the edge of the surface; practice on cardboard to get a feel for the technique. If the brush doesn't hold its point or spreads out too far, try turning it slightly as you draw it along. This will re-form the brush as you work.

For double stripes or designs with more than one color, let each stripe dry completely before you paint the next one. Work from the inside stripe out to avoid smudging.

Taped Striping. On long edges, or for wide stripes, use masking tape to define the stripes. The surface must be clean, with all wax and dirt removed. Carefully

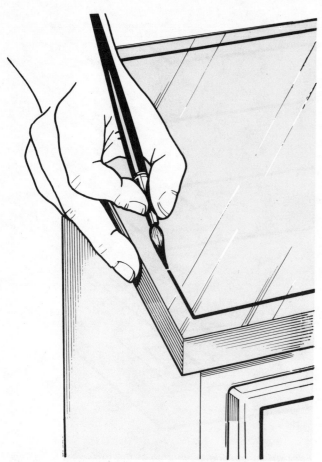

To make a freehand stripe, draw your hand along the edge of the surface to hold the brush steady along the top.

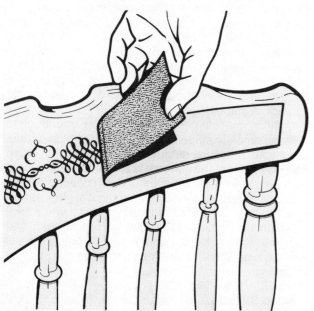

Soak the decal in warm water until the paper backing loosens; then smooth it into place and peel off the backing.

press the tape along the surface; make sure it's straight, and at a consistent distance from the edge. Seal the edges of the tape carefully to keep the paint from seeping under it; press each tape edge firmly all along its length with your thumbnail or the tip of a putty knife.

Apply the enamel with a good-quality artists' brush, roughly the same width as the masked stripe. Use enough paint to cover the surface completely, but smooth it out well; don't let the stripe get thick or uneven. Let the paint dry completely; then remove the tape, pulling it gently away from the surface. Do *not* leave the tape on the surface for more than 12 hours, or it may damage the finish.

For double stripes or designs with more than one color, let each stripe dry completely before you tape the next one. Apply tape very carefully where stripes cross, to keep it from damaging the earlier stripes. Work from the inside of the surface toward the edges.

Protecting the Surface. To prevent damage to the stripes, the surface should be sealed with varnish. Apply the varnish directly over the stripes, as detailed in Chapter 6.

DECALS

On informal furniture, decals can add a down-home, cheerful touch. They shouldn't be used on expensive furniture, but they look right at home on some early American reproductions, and Pennsylvania Dutch decals or other country-look designs can be very attractive on kitchen furniture or in a child's room. Home center and hardware stores often carry decals, but you'll probably find a better selection at a craft or art supply store.

How to Apply Decals. A surface to be decorated with decals must be clean; remove all wax and dirt. Decals consist of a painted or printed image on a varnished or lacquered paper base. To apply a decal, soak it in warm water until the paper loosens; then carefully smooth the decal onto the surface to be decorated and peel off the backing paper. Follow any specific instructions provided by the manufacturer.

If you don't like the effect of a decal, or if it isn't positioned correctly, peel it off while it's still wet, dip it into warm water again, and reapply it. To remove dry decals, buy special decal-removing strips. Soak the remover strip in warm water, as directed by the manufacturer, and place it over the decal to be removed. Let it set for about 30 minutes, or as directed, and then peel it off; the decal will come with it.

Protecting the Surface. To prevent damage to the decals, the surface should be sealed with varnish. Apply the varnish directly over the decals, as detailed in Chapter 6.

Chapter 8
Working With Unfinished Furniture

If you're willing to spend a little time on it, unfinished furniture can be a real buy. Home centers, general merchandise outlets, and specialized stores sell all types of unfinished furniture, often completely assembled—tables, chairs, desks, dressers, cabinets, and shelves. Sometimes this furniture is well worth buying; sometimes it isn't. If you know what to look for and how to deal with it, you can turn these assembly-line pieces into solid, good-looking, professionally finished furniture.

BUYING: WHAT TO LOOK FOR

Out of all the different types and styles of unfinished furniture, how do you know which pieces are worth buying? Price, unfortunately, is the first indicator; you really get what you pay for with this furniture. Before you buy any unfinished piece, do a little comparison-shopping to get an idea of what's available. Most unfinished furniture is pine, but some is made with other woods. Whatever type of wood is used, the quality of the wood and the workmanship that goes into the piece can vary tremendously.

When you find a piece of furniture you like, take a good look at it. Is the wood clear or full of knots, smooth or rough? Cheap furniture is usually knotty and sap-streaked; the more expensive pieces are made with better-quality wood. What state is the wood in? Cheap furniture is probably raw, and may have rough edges and deep saw gouges. Good unfinished furniture is often already sanded, ready for finishing.

Another important consideration is how well the piece of furniture is made. Most unfinished furniture is assembled with staples driven by a power staple gun; unless the stapling is carefully done, the joints may not be secure. How sturdy is the piece? Does it have wobbly legs, or are parts of it poorly fastened together? You can fix loose joints, but it's hard to salvage a piece that's badly matched or falling apart completely.

Are doors and drawers aligned properly, and do they work smoothly? If they don't, is it because they're the wrong size for the opening or because of loosely or inaccurately fastened hardware or drawer guides? You can deal with mechanical problems, but a part that's too big or too small can never be adjusted. Examine all moving parts to make sure they're cut, joined, and assembled properly—finishing can do a lot, but it can't remake a shoddy piece.

Finally, look at the style. Do you like the lines of the piece? Will it do the job you want it for? Don't settle for a piece of furniture that's the wrong size or style; it isn't worth working on something you don't really want. On the other hand, a piece of furniture that's basically right can be given any character you like with different

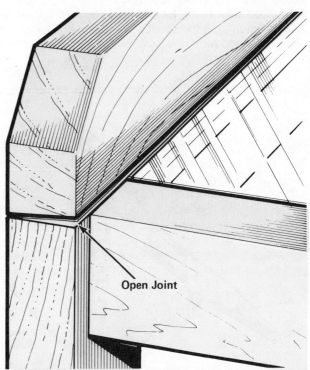

Examine the joints to make sure they're well matched and fastened; gaps between pieces are hard to deal with.

Open Joint

hardware, trim moldings, decorations, or special finishes.

Before you make a final decision, assess the work you'll have to do to get the piece ready to finish—cleaning out knotholes and sap pockets, regluing legs, renailing drawers, repairing splits, smoothing splintered edges, changing hardware. How much time and effort will it take? How much hardware and trim will you have to add? Are the size and style right? Do you like the wood? How much are you saving by buying the piece unfinished? It all comes down to one basic question: is it worth it? If you choose carefully, it is.

HOW TO DEAL WITH THE PROBLEMS

No matter how carefully you shop, unfinished furniture is likely to have a few problems. The joints may be loose; moving parts may stick. There are usually a few knots in the wood, and these will bleed through the finish if they aren't sealed. There are almost always rough edges or saw marks. Before you prepare the wood for finishing, take the time to deal with these problems. Your results will more than justify the effort.

Loose Joinery and Poor Assembly. The first step in working with unfinished furniture is making sure it's solid. Examine the joints to locate any weak points; drawers are especially likely to need refastening. If the staples or other fasteners are solid, renailing may not be needed, but if they're off-center or don't look very secure, reinforce them by driving finishing nails next to them. Drill pilot holes for the nails to keep the wood from splintering. If the staples are loose, pull them out with pliers, and renail the joint. Fill the staple holes with wood plastic.

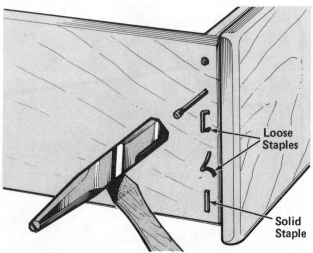

In stapled joints, drive nails to secure weak points where staples are loose or missing; leave well-driven staples in place. Fill the staple holes with wood plastic.

Loose legs, rungs, arms, or spindles should be reglued, as detailed in Chapter 10, "Structural Repairs." Test all parts of the piece to make sure they're secure, and reglue or refasten any loose part.

If the piece has drawers, they should work smoothly. Check the drawer guides, inside the frame, and the runners on the bottom edges of the drawer; they should be square and securely fastened, with no protruding nail heads. Refasten the guides or runners, if necessary, and countersink protruding nail heads with a nail set.

Knots and Sap Pockets. Examine the wood carefully for spots where sap has flowed or resin beaded on the surface. Scrape off hardened resin, and clean knots and sap pockets with turpentine on a soft cloth. If large knots are loose, remove them entirely; then apply carpenters' glue around the edges and replace the knots, flush with the surface. If small knots are loose—pin knots—remove them completely and fill the holes with wood plastic or water putty. Seal all knots and sap pockets with a coat of 1-pound-cut white shellac; if the shellac is completely absorbed, apply two or more coats, as needed, to seal the knots completely.

Rough Edges. To correct surface roughness, sand the edge smooth. If there are low spots or gaps in an edge, fill them with wood plastic or water putty and then sand the filler smooth. Square edges should be very slightly rounded before finishing; smooth and round them with fine-grit sandpaper on a sanding block. Do *not* plane edges; planing could splinter the wood.

Saw Notches and Splinters. Dull saw blades leave notches and splinters, and you're likely to find these problems anywhere the wood has been cut or joined. If the notches are very shallow, you may be able to sand them out. In most cases, you'll have to fill them with wood plastic, and then sand the filler smooth.

SPECIAL FINISHING STEPS

Unfinished furniture requires the same preparation and finishing as stripped furniture, but it also requires a few preliminary steps. First, sand the wood very thoroughly. Unfinished pieces are usually rougher than stripped pieces; start sanding with medium-grit sandpaper and then work up to fine-grit. Make sure all edges, knot faces, joints, and door and drawer interiors are completely smooth.

Raw wood must be carefully sealed; unsealed wood absorbs moisture, and this can cause serious problems. If the piece of furniture has drawers, seal them inside and out with a coat of thinned white shellac or sanding sealer, to prevent warping and splitting. Seal all hidden parts—drawer guides, side and bottom panels, and any other exposed wood. Seal the entire piece of furniture, and then lightly sand it again to re-

Pin knots should be removed completely so they don't work loose after finishing. Pry out the knot with a knife, and fill and seal the hole.

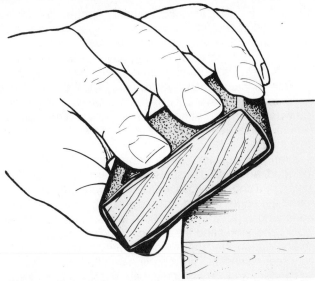

All square edges should be very slightly rounded. Smooth and blunt them carefully with fine-grit sandpaper on a sanding block; do not use a plane.

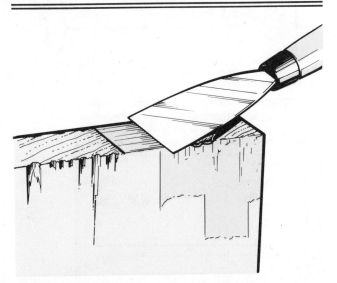

Dull saw blades leave notched and splintered edges. To fix them, fill the splintered edges with wood plastic, and sand the filler smooth.

You can simulate age by battering the entire piece of furniture lightly and evenly with a piece of 1x3 studded with flatheaded tacks.

move any tooth from the surface. Further finishing can be done as detailed in Chapters 5 and 6.

INSTANT AGING: DISTRESSING THE WOOD

Properly prepared and finished, unfinished furniture usually looks exactly like what it is: brand-new. If you want a piece of furniture to look well-worn, you can achieve the illusion of age with the technique of distressing. This should be done before the final smoothing and finishing.

Basically, distressing is adding the effects of years of wear and tear in just a few minutes. Old furniture usually has dents, dings, and worn edges; rungs may be flattened, chair seats smoothed down, or corners blunted. You can add the dents by pounding the wood, wear down the edges by rasping and sanding, and provide every appearance of long use. The real trick of distressing is knowing when to stop—what you want is a subtle effect of wear, not an obviously battered look. Distressing can be particularly effective under an antiqued finish.

General wear and tear is easy to imitate. Use the rounded end of a ball-peen hammer to make random dents in the surface. For overall battering, drive flatheaded tacks into a piece of 1 × 3, leaving the heads protruding slightly; pound the wood lightly and evenly. Large, shallow dents can be made with a large, smooth rock. With any distressing tool, exercise a little restraint; if you hit the wood too hard, you'll end up with splits and splinters. Work in random strokes; don't mark the wood in any set pattern, such as rows. What you're aiming at is a general dulling or blunting of the brand-new look.

Over years of use, sharp edges gradually become rounded, and high-use spots—chair arms or rungs, for instance—show obvious wear. To produce this effect, round the edges of tops, drawer and cabinet fronts, and arms and legs with a medium-grit sandpaper on a block, and then sand the rounded surface smooth. On chairs, flatten the front rung slightly where you'd rest your feet against it. This rounding and flattening should be random and very gradual, with no obvious pattern; add noticeable wear only to the natural high-use spots. Absolutely even wear doesn't happen naturally, and it shouldn't be forced with distressing—envision normal wear, and aim at this effect.

Very old furniture sometimes has worm holes, usually near a leg. Poorly faked worm holes are very obvious, but it isn't hard to make not-so-obvious fakes. To get the wormholed effect, make a few holes in strategic spots with the point of an ice pick. Drive the pick in to varying depths, so the holes are not all the same diameter and depth, and don't overdo it. A few holes can be convincing, but holes on the entire piece won't fool anybody.

When you've achieved the look—or the degree of wear—you want, go over the distressed wood lightly with fine-grit sandpaper. Smooth out any obvious rough edges or splinters, but be careful not to remove the marks of distressing. Then finish the piece.

DECORATING: THE FINAL TOUCHES

Before you finish the piece of furniture, you can add decorative moldings or carvings to dress it up. This obviously isn't necessary if you like the design of the piece as it is, but if you want a more ornate look, decorations can be very effective. Decorative hardwood moldings and ready-to-finish carvings are available in many designs; look for them at paint and hobby stores or order from a woodworking supply company. Attach wood decorations with brads or glue them into place; stain and finish them to match.

After you finish the piece, you can dress it up with new hardware—brass hinges, china and brass drawer pulls, any type of hardware you like. Good hardware can be expensive, but it can do a lot for an otherwise undistinguished piece of furniture. For other special looks, consider the effects of antiquing, flyspecking, gilding, or striping; or add decals or stencils. Special-effects finishes are detailed in Chapter 7.

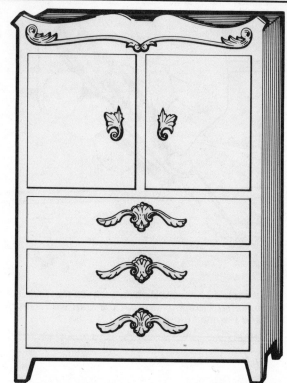

For a more elaborate or "antique" look, add decorative hardwood carvings, attached with glue or brads and stained and finished to match.

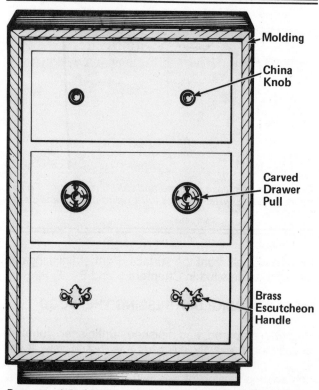

Molding

China Knob

Carved Drawer Pull

Brass Escutcheon Handle

Dress up plain furniture with new hardware—brass, wood, or china, in any style you like. Hardwood molding adds distinction.

Chapter 9
Surface Repairs

Old or new, furniture often shows evidence of hard service: stains, scratches, burns, and all the other signs of use and abuse. Veneer may be loose or broken; hardware may be missing; the wood may be discolored. Unless the damage is severe or extensive, most of these problems are easy to deal with.

Surface repairs aren't difficult, but it can be hard to tell what you're getting into. If only the surface is affected, the damage is usually easy to repair; if the wood is damaged too, you may have to refinish part or all of the piece. Unless it's obvious that refinishing is needed, start with the simplest technique and work up.

BASIC RESTORATION TECHNIQUES

Most finishes protect the wood surface by forming a protective coating. To repair a damaged finish coating, work only to the depth that it's affected. If you must remove the entire thickness of the finish, or if the damage extends into the wood under the finish, you'll find yourself involved in spot refinishing—an unpredictable technique, and not always a successful one, especially where staining is necessary. On any surface, work carefully, and don't remove more of the finish than you have to.

Stains and Discoloration

White Spots. Shellac and lacquer finishes are not resistant to water and alcohol; spills and condensation from glasses can leave permanent white spots or rings on these finishes. To remove these white spots, first try polishing the surface with liquid furniture polish; buff the surface firmly. If this doesn't work, lightly wipe the stained surface with denatured alcohol. Use as little alcohol as possible; too much will damage the finish.

If neither polishing nor alcohol treatment removes the white spots, the damaged finish must be treated with abrasives. For a very gentle abrasive, mix cigarette ashes to a paste with a few drops of vegetable oil, light mineral oil, or linseed oil. Rub the ash-oil paste over the stained area, along the grain of the wood, and then wipe the surface clean with a soft cloth. If necessary, repeat the procedure; stubborn spots may require several applications. Then wax and polish the entire surface.

If rubbing with ashes is not effective, go over the stained area with a mixture of rottenstone and linseed oil. Mix the rottenstone and oil to a thin paste, and rub the paste gently over the stain, along the grain of the wood. Rottenstone is a fast-cutting abrasive, so rub very carefully, and check the surface frequently to make sure you aren't cutting too deep. As soon as the white spots disappear, stop rubbing and wipe the wood clean with a soft cloth. Then apply two coats of hard furniture wax and buff the wood to a shine.

Blushing. Blushing, a white haze over a large surface or an entire piece of furniture, is a common problem with old shellac and lacquer finishes. The discoloration is caused by moisture, and it can sometimes be removed the same way white spots are removed. Buff the surface lightly and evenly with No. 0000 steel wool dipped in linseed oil; work with the grain of the wood, rubbing evenly on the entire surface, until the white haze disappears. Then wipe the wood clean with a soft cloth, apply two coats of hard furniture wax, and buff the surface to a shine.

Blushing can sometimes be removed by reamalgamation, as detailed in Chapter 3, "Restoring the Old Finish." If the surface is crazed or alligatored, reamalgamation should be used instead of steel-wool rubbing. If neither rubbing nor reamalgamation removes the haze, the piece of furniture must be refinished.

Black Spots. Black spots are caused by water that has penetrated the finish completely and entered the wood. They cannot be removed without damage to the finish. If the spots are on a clearly defined surface, you may be able to remove the finish from this surface only; otherwise, the entire piece of furniture will have to be stripped, as detailed in Chapter 4. When the finish has been removed, bleach the entire stained surface with a solution of oxalic acid, as detailed in Chapter 5, "Preparing the Wood." Then refinish as necessary.

Ink Stains. Ink stains that have penetrated the finish, like black water spots, cannot be removed without refinishing. Less serious ink stains can sometimes be removed. Lightly buff the stained area with a cloth moistened with mineral spirits; then rinse the wood with clean water on a soft cloth. Dry the surface thoroughly, and then wax and polish it.

If this does not remove the ink, lightly rub the stained area, along the grain of the wood, with No. 0000 steel wool moistened with mineral spirits. Then wipe the

Spot-staining is tricky, but it is sometimes successful. Apply stain to the repair area with an artists' brush.

surface clean and wax and polish it. This treatment may damage the finish; if necessary, refinish the damaged spot as discussed below. If the area is badly damaged, the entire surface or piece of furniture will have to be refinished.

Grease, Tar, Paint, Crayon, and Lipstick Spots. These spots usually affect only the surface of the finish. To remove wet paint, use the appropriate solvent on a soft cloth—mineral spirits for oil-base paint, water for latex paint. To remove dry paint or other materials, very carefully lift the surface residue with the edge of a putty knife. Do *not* scrape the wood, or you'll scratch the finish. When the surface material has been removed, buff the area very lightly along the grain of the wood with No. 0000 steel wool moistened with mineral spirits. Then wax and polish the entire surface.

Wax and Gum Spots. Wax and gum usually come off quickly, but they must be removed carefully to prevent damage to the finish. To make the wax or gum brittle, press it with a packet of ice wrapped in a towel or paper towel. Let the deposit harden; then lift it off with your thumbnail. The hardened wax or gum should pop off the surface with very little pressure. If necessary, repeat the ice application. Do *not* scrape the deposit off, or you'll scratch the finish.

When the wax or gum is completely removed, buff the area very lightly along the grain of the wood with No. 0000 steel wool moistened with mineral spirits. Then wax and polish the entire surface.

Spot Refinishing

Any repair that involves removing the damaged finish completely—deep scratches, gouges, burns, or any other damage—also involves refinishing the repair area. Spot refinishing is not always easy, and it's not always successful, especially on stained surfaces. If the damage isn't too bad, it's worth trying. If you'll have to touch up several areas on one surface, you're probably better off refinishing the surface or the piece of furniture completely.

To stain one area on a surface, use an oil-based stain that matches the surrounding stain. See Chapter 5, "Preparing the Wood," for staining technique. You may have to mix stains to get a good match. Test the stain on an inconspicuous unfinished part of the wood before working on the finished surface.

Before applying the stain, prepare the damaged area for finishing, as detailed in Chapter 5. Sealing is not necessary. Apply the stain to the damaged area with an artists' brush or a clean cloth, covering the entire bare area. Let the stain set for 15 minutes and then wipe it off with a clean cloth. If the color is too light, apply another coat of stain, wait 15 minutes, and wipe again. Repeat this procedure until you're satisfied with the color; then let the stain dry according to the manufacturer's instructions.

Lightly buff the stained surface with No. 0000 steel wool, and wipe it clean with a tack cloth. Apply a new coat of the same finish already on the surface—varnish, penetrating resin, shellac, or lacquer—over the newly stained area, feathering out the new finish into the surrounding old finish. Let the new finish dry for one to two days, and lightly buff the patched area with No. 0000 steel wool. Finally, wax the entire surface with hard paste wax, and polish it to a shine.

Surface Damage

Scratches. To hide small scratches quickly, break the meat of a walnut, pecan, or Brazil nut and rub it along the scratch. The oil in the nut meat will darken the raw scratch.

Where many shallow scratches are present, apply hard paste wax to the surface with No. 0000 steel wool, stroking very lightly along the grain of the wood. Then buff the surface with a soft cloth. For shallow scratches on an otherwise sound shellac or lacquer finish, reamalgamation can be used to restore the finish, as detailed in Chapter 3.

For one or two deeper scratches, furniture-patching wax sticks are usually effective. These retouching sticks, made in several wood colors, are available at hardware and sometimes grocery stores; choose a stick to match the finish. To use the wax stick, run it firmly along the scratch, applying enough pressure to fill the scratch with wax. Remove any excess wax with the edge of a credit card or other thin plastic card. Let the wax dry; then buff with a soft cloth.

Badly scratched surfaces should usually be re-finished, but to hide one or two very deep scratches, you may be able to stain the raw area to match, as detailed above. Apply oil-based stain with an artists' brush, drawing it carefully along the scratch; let it stand for 15 minutes and wipe it off. If necessary, repeat this procedure until the scratch matches the rest of the wood. Let the area dry completely, as directed by the stain manufacturer; then apply hard paste wax and buff the waxed surface to a shine.

Dings. Dings are tiny chips in the finish, usually caused by a sharp blow. The wood may not be affected. To repair a ding, use a sharp craft knife to remove any loose finish in or around the ding. Work carefully, scraping the damaged spot with the flat, sharp edge of the knife blade; do *not* scratch the spot. Then very carefully feather the edges of the ding with No. 0000 steel wool.

Clean the ding area with a soft cloth moistened in mineral spirits, and let it dry completely. Then, with an artists' brush, carefully apply new finish to the spot—varnish, shellac, lacquer, or enamel—to match the rest of the finish. The spot will be very noticeable at first. Let the finish dry; it will be glossy. Then lightly buff the spot with No. 0000 steel wool, and wax and polish the entire piece of furniture. The ding should blend perfectly when the job is complete.

Dents. Small, shallow dents in pine and other soft woods are usually easy to remove; large and deep dents, especially in hard wood, are harder to repair. Dents are easiest to remove from bare wood. Very large, shallow dents are probably best left untreated. Very deep dents should be filled, as detailed below for cracks and gouges.

On finished surfaces, you'll have to remove the finish around the damaged area. Using fine-grit sandpaper, carefully remove the finish for about ½ inch around the spot. To raise the wood in the dent, apply a few drops of water to the dent and let the water penetrate the wood for a day or so. Do *not* wet the entire surface. This treatment may be enough to raise the dent, especially if the dent is shallow and the wood is soft.

If this doesn't raise the dent, soak a cloth in water and wring it out. Place the damp cloth, folded in several layers, over the dent; then press the cloth firmly with a warm iron. Be careful not to touch the iron directly to the wood. This moist heat may be enough to swell the wood and raise the dent. If it isn't, apply a commercial wood-swelling liquid to the area and give it time to work—about a day or so, as directed by the manufacturer.

For deep dents that can't be raised with water, heat, or wood sweller, use a fine straight pin or needle to drive a series of holes in the dent. Pound the straight pin in about ¼ inch, and carefully pull it out with pliers; the holes should be as small as possible. Then treat

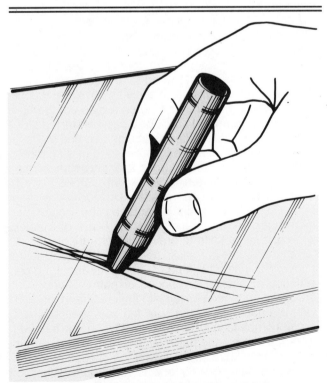

Wax furniture-patching sticks can be used to hide fairly deep scratches; press the stick firmly to fill the scratch.

Use a fine pin or needle to drive a series of small holes in a stubborn dent; then swell the wood to raise the dent.

the dent as above. The pinholes let the water penetrate the wood's surface, and if you're careful, they won't show when the wood has been raised.

After the dent has been raised, let the wood dry for about a week, and then refinish the damaged area as above. Let the finish dry completely. Lightly buff the new finish with No. 0000 steel wool, and then wax and polish the entire surface.

Cracks and Gouges. Cracks and gouges should be filled so that they're level with the surface of the wood. For very small holes, like staple holes, wood-tone putty sticks can be used. If you can't match the wood, several colors can be mixed together. To use a putty stick, wipe it across the hole and smooth the surface with your finger. If you plan to finish or refinish the wood, let the putty dry for at least a week before proceeding further.

For larger holes, wood plastic and water putty are the easiest fillers. These fillers can be used on bare or finished wood; wood plastic is available in several colors, and water putty can be tinted with oil or water stain. However, wood plastic and water putty patches

Fill deep cracks and gouges with wood plastic or water putty; leave the filler slightly high to allow for shrinkage as it dries. When the patch is dry, sand it smooth.

are usually noticeable, and may look darker than the wood. For the best results, test the patch on an inconspicuous surface to make sure the color is right.

To use wood plastic, carefully clean the crack or gouge with the tip of a craft knife, and then press the plastic firmly in with the tip of a craft knife or the edge of a putty knife. Wood plastic shrinks slightly as it dries, so press it in tightly and leave it mounded slightly above the surface of the wood.

Wood plastic dries fairly quickly, but let it set for at least two days. Then smooth the patch lightly with fine-grit sandpaper and buff the area with No. 0000 steel wool. If surrounding finish is involved, feather the edges so that the new patch blends in with it. Then, if necessary, stain the patch and buff it lightly with No. 0000 steel wool. Apply finish to match the rest of the surface, using an artists' brush and feathering the edges. Let the finish dry and then lightly buff it with No. 0000 steel wool; clean the area of any residue, and wax and polish the surface.

Water putty dries flint-hard, usually harder than the wood being patched. It's best used on bare wood. Water putty can be toned with oil and water stains, but you'll have to experiment to come up with a perfect match. To use water putty, mix the powder with water to the consistency of putty; then trowel it into the break with a putty knife, leaving the patch slightly high. Let the patch dry completely, and sand and steel-wool the area smooth and level with the surrounding surface. Finish the surface as above, or finish the entire piece of furniture.

For the most professional patching job, use shellac sticks to fill cracks and gouges. Shellac sticks leave the least conspicuous patch, and are very effective on finished wood that's in good condition. Shellac sticks are available in several wood-tone colors; use a stick that matches the finish as closely as possible. Practice on scrap wood before working on a piece of furniture.

Carefully clean the crack or gouge with the tip of a craft knife. Shellac sticks must be heated and melted to fill the crack. The best heat source for this is an alcohol lamp or a propane torch turned to a low setting. Do not use a match to soften the stick; the smoke from the match may discolor the shellac. Do not use a range burner; liquid shellac could damage either gas or electric ranges. Hold the stick over the blade of a palette knife or a putty knife to prevent it from dripping.

To use a shellac stick, hold it to the heat source above the knife, until it has softened to about the consistency of glazing compound or putty. Then quickly press the softened shellac into the crack and smooth it with the hot knife. Make sure the soft shellac fills the break completely; it hardens quickly, so you'll have to work fast. Leave the patch slightly high. Then, with the heated putty knife blade, trowel the shellac smooth.

Let the patch set for one to two hours. When the shellac is hard, plane or sand the surface smooth and level. The finish surrounding the break usually doesn't

Heat the shellac stick over an alcohol lamp or a propane torch, holding a palette or putty knife between the stick and the flame to keep it from dripping.

When the shellac has softened to the consistency of putty, quickly press it into the crack, smoothing it in with the hot knife. Leave the patch slightly high.

have to be retouched, but the surface can be coated with shellac, if desired. Apply the shellac finish as detailed in Chapter 6. To make the shellac match a satin-gloss finish, rub the surface smooth with No. 0000 steel wool and linseed oil.

To fill very deep holes, use wood plastic or water putty to fill the hole almost level. Let the filler dry completely, and then fill the indentation with a shellac stick.

If a hole or split is very large, don't overlook the possibility of filling it with a piece of wood cut and trimmed to fit perfectly. If the patching wood can be taken from the piece of furniture in a spot that won't show, the repair may be almost impossible to detect.

Fit the wood patch into the hole or split; use carpenters' glue to bond it to the surrounding wood. Leave the patch slightly high. When the glue is completely dry, sand the plug smoothly level with the surface of the surrounding wood. Then refinish the piece of furniture.

Burns. Burns on furniture can range from scorches to deep char, but the usual problem is cigarette burns. Scorches from cigarettes or cigars are usually the easiest to remove. Buff the scorched area with a fine steel wool pad moistened with mineral spirits until the scorch disappears. Then wipe it clean and wax and polish the surface.

More serious burns require the removal of the charred wood. Shallow burns, when repaired, will always leave a slight indentation in the wood, but this depression will not be conspicuous. Deep burn holes can be filled, as detailed above.

First, remove the damaged wood. With the flat sharp edge of a craft knife, very carefully scrape away the charred wood. For deep burns, use a curved blade. Do *not* scratch the burn area. Scrape away the char right to the bare wood, feathering out the edges. Any burned or scorched spots will show, so all the burn crust must be removed. Work carefully to avoid scratching the wood with the point of the knife.

If the surface is veneer, you must be *very* careful not to scrape through the veneer into the wood core. If the burn is deep enough to go through the veneer, the hole will have to be filled to the level of the core wood. The veneer will have to be patched, as detailed below.

When the charred wood has been completely removed, lightly sand the edges of the groove or trench to level it with the surrounding surface as much as possible. Press lightly into the groove with fine-grit sandpaper, removing only the char from the burned area; be careful not to damage the surrounding finish. If you're not sure all the burn has been removed, wet the sanded area. If water makes the burned area look

To remove a burn spot, scrape away the charred wood with a craft knife; feather the edges of the depression.

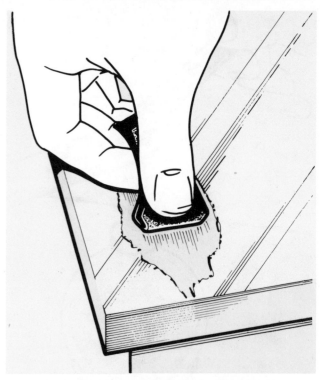

After removing the char, sand the burn area lightly to smooth it and level it out to the surrounding surface.

burned again, you haven't removed all the char.

With deep burns, the groove left after the char is removed will probably be quite noticeable. Level the groove as much as possible with fine-grit sandpaper, but stay close to the edges of the groove. If you sand too far out from the burn area, the damaged area will be very visible as a wide saucer-shaped indentation. If the depression isn't too deep, try swelling the wood as detailed above for dents. If you're left with a deep gouge, the burn area can be filled with wood plastic or a shellac stick, as above.

After smoothing out the burn, refinish the damaged area as above. Let the new finish dry for one or two days, and then lightly buff the patch with No. 0000 steel wool to blend the edges into the old finish. Finally, wax and polish the entire piece of furniture.

HOW TO REPAIR VENEER

Because veneer is only a thin layer of wood, attached with glue to a solid base, it is very vulnerable to damage. On old furniture, the glue that holds the veneer is often not water-resistant. Prolonged humidity or exposure to water can soften the glue, letting the veneer blister, crack, or peel. Veneer is also easily damaged from the surface, and old veneers are often cracked, buckled, or broken, with chips or entire pieces missing.

In most cases, as long as the veneer layer is basi-

cally in good shape, the thinness that makes it damage-prone also makes it easy to repair. Undamaged veneer can be reglued; chips and bare spots can be filled with matching veneer. If you're careful to match the grain the repairs will hardly show.

Blisters. Small blisters in veneer can usually be flattened with heat. To protect the surface, set a sheet of wax paper and then a sheet of smooth cardboard on the surface, and cover the cardboard with a clean cloth. Press the blistered area firmly with a medium-hot iron; if there are several blisters, move the iron slowly and evenly back and forth. Be careful not to touch the exposed surface with the iron. Check the surface every few minutes or so as you work, and stop pressing as soon as the blisters have flattened. Leaving the cardboard in place, weight the repair area solidly for 24 hours. Then wax and polish the surface.

Large blisters must usually be slit, because the veneer has swelled. With a sharp craft knife or single-edge razor blade, carefully cut the blister open down the middle, along the grain of the wood. Be careful not to cut into the base wood. Then cover the surface and apply heat as above, checking every few seconds as the glue softens; if the glue has deteriorated and does not soften, carefully scrape it out and insert a little carpenters' glue under the slit edges of the bubble with the tip of the knife. Be careful not to use too much glue; if necessary, wipe off any excess as the blister flattens. As soon as one edge of the slit bubble overlaps the other, carefully shave off the overlapping edge with a craft knife or razor blade. Heat the blister again; if the edges overlap further, shave the overlapping edge again. When the blister is completely flattened, weight the repair area solidly for 24 hours. Then wax and polish the entire surface.

Loose Veneer. Lifted veneer occurs most often at the corners of tabletops, on cabinet and dresser edges, legs, and drawer fronts. If the loose veneer is undamaged, it can be reglued.

First, remove the residue of old glue left on the back of the veneer and on the base wood. With a sharp craft knife or razor blade, carefully scrape out as much of the old glue as possible. Don't lift the veneer any further; if you bend it up, you'll damage it. After scraping out as much old glue as you can, clean the bonding surfaces with benzene or naphtha to remove any residue; glue left under the loose area will interfere with the new adhesive. If any glue still remains, sand the bonding surfaces lightly with fine-grit sandpaper, and then wipe them clean with a soft cloth moistened with mineral spirits. If more than one veneer layer is loose, clean each layer the same way.

The veneer can be reattached with contact cement, but you may prefer to use carpenters' glue because it sets more slowly and allows repositioning. To reglue the veneer, apply contact cement to both bonding surfaces and let it set, as directed by the manufacturer; if necessary, set a small tack or two between the layers to keep them from touching. Or apply carpenters' glue to the base wood, spreading it on along the grain with

a small brush. Then, starting at the solidly attached veneer and working out toward the loose edge, smooth the loose veneer carefully into place. Contact cement bonds immediately, so make sure the veneer is exactly matched; if you're using carpenters' glue, press from the center out to force out any excess, and wipe the excess off immediately. If more than one veneer layer is loose, work from the bottom up to reglue each layer.

Reglued veneer, whatever adhesive is used, should be clamped or weighted. To protect the surface, cover it with a sheet of wax paper; make sure all excess glue is removed. Set a buffer block of scrap wood over the newly glued area, and use another block or a soft cloth to protect the opposite edge or side of the surface. Clamp the glued and protected surface firmly with C-clamps or hand screws, for one to two days. Then remove the clamps and the buffers, and wax and polish the entire surface.

Cracked or Broken Veneer. If the veneer is lifted and cracked, but not broken completely through, it can be reglued as above; large areas may be easier to repair if you break the veneer off along the cracks. Broken veneer can be reglued, but you must be very careful not to damage the edges of the break. Do *not* trim ragged edges; an irregular mend line will not be as visible as a perfectly straight line.

Before applying glue to the veneer, clean the bonding surfaces carefully, as above. Fit the broken edges carefully together to make sure they match perfectly. Then apply contact cement to both surfaces, or spread carpenters' glue on the base wood. Set the broken veneer carefully into place, matching the edges exactly, and press firmly to knit the broken edges to-

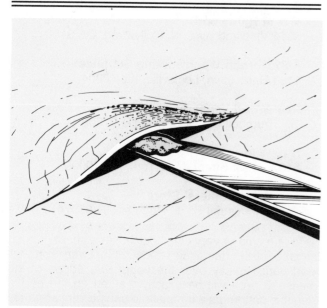

To repair a large blister in veneer, slit it and insert a little glue under the edges; then flatten it with heat.

Loose veneer can be reglued. Apply glue to the base wood, press the veneer into place, and clamp it firmly.

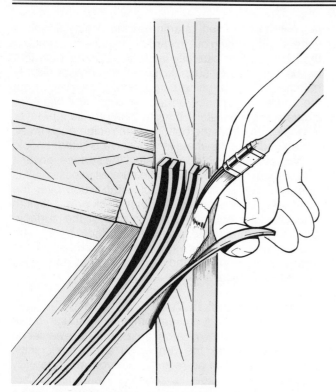

When more than one layer has separated, work from the bottom up, from the inside out, to reglue each layer.

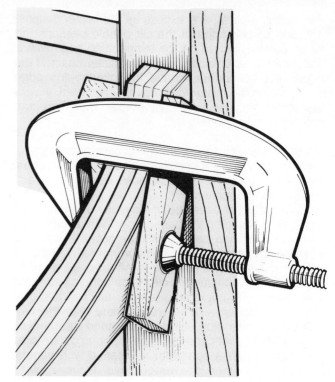

Press the reglued layers together to align them properly; wipe off excess glue. Then clamp the mended part securely.

gether. Clamp the mended area as above. Refinishing may be necessary when the mend is complete; if so, use a non-wash-away paint and varnish remover, and treat the veneered surface very gently.

Chipped or Missing Veneer. Replacing veneer is easy, but finding a new piece to replace it may not be. If the piece of furniture is not valuable, you may be able to take the patch from a part of it that won't show. The patch area must be along an edge, so that you can lift the veneer with a craft knife or a stiff-bladed putty knife.

In most cases, patch veneer should not be taken from the same piece of furniture; you'll have to buy matching veneer to make the repair. If only a small piece is missing, you may be able to fill in the hole with veneer edging tape, sold at many home centers and lumberyards. Or, if you have access to junk furniture, you may be able to salvage a similar veneer from another piece of furniture. For larger patches, or if you can't find a scrap piece of matching veneer, buy a sheet of matching veneer from a specialized wood supplier, locally or by mail. National suppliers include:

Robert M. Albrecht
18701 Barthenia, Northridge, CA 91324

Constantine & Son
2050 Eastchester Rd., Bronx, NY 10461

Craftsman Wood Service
1735 W. Courtland Ct., Addison, IL 60101

Exotic Woodshed
65 N. York Rd., Warminster, PA 18974

M & M Hardwood
5344 Vineland Ave., N. Hollywood, CA 91601

Bob Morgan Woodworking Supplies
1123 Bardstown, Louisville, KY 40204

Real Wood Veneers
107 Trumbull St., Elizabeth, NJ 07206

H.L. Wild
510 E. 11th Street, New York, NY 10009

The Woodworkers' Store
21801 Industrial Blvd., Rogers, MN 55374

To fit a chip or very small patch, set a sheet of bond paper over the damaged veneer. Rub a very soft, dull lead pencil gently over the paper; the edges of the damaged area will be exactly marked on the paper. Use this pattern as a template to cut the veneer patch. Tape the pattern to the patching wood, matching the grain of the new veneer to the grain of the damaged

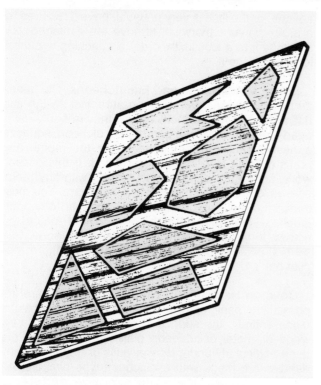

To mend veneer, cut a patch in an irregular shape; any of these shapes will be less visible than a square.

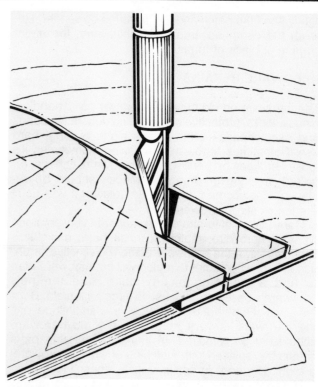

With the patch veneer held firmly over the damaged area, cut through the patching sheet and the veneer below it.

area. Cut the patch firmly and carefully with a sharp craft knife; it's better to make it too big than too small.

To make a larger patch, tape the patching veneer firmly over the damaged area with masking tape, with the grain and pattern of the patch matching the grain and pattern of the damaged veneer. Make sure the patch is flat against the surface, and securely held in place. Cut the patch in an irregular shape, as illustrated, or in a boat or shield shape; these shapes will be less visible than a square or rectangular patch would be. Cut the patch carefully with a craft knife, scoring through the patching veneer and through the damaged veneer layer below it.

Untape the patching sheet and pop out the patch. With the tip of the craft knife, remove the cut-out patch of damaged veneer; if necessary, score it and remove it in pieces. Be very careful not to damage the edges of the patch area. Remove only the top veneer layer; do not cut into the base wood. Remove any old glue and clean the base wood as above.

Test the fit of the patch in the hole. It should fit exactly, flush with the surrounding surface, with no gaps or overlaps. If the patch is too big or too thick, do *not* force it in. Carefully sand the edges or the back with fine-grit sandpaper to fit it to the hole.

Glue the fitted patch into place with contact cement or carpenters' glue, as above, and clamp or weight it solidly. Let the repair dry for one to two days; then very

Before gluing the patch in, test it for fit; it should fit exactly, flush with the surrounding surface, with no gaps.

lightly sand the patch and the surrounding veneer. Refinish the damaged area or, if necessary, the entire surface or piece of furniture.

HARDWARE REPAIRS

The hardware on old furniture—drawer pulls, handles, hinges, locks, protective corners, and decorative bands and escutcheons—often shows signs of long, hard use. Sometimes hardware is missing; sometimes it's loose, broken, or bent. Loose hardware can be repaired; missing or damaged pieces should be replaced. Replacement is also the solution if you don't like the existing hardware.

Many pieces of furniture are made with very common types of hardware; matching these basic designs is fairly simple. If the hardware is more distinctive or unusual, it may be easier to replace all the hardware than to find a matching piece; make sure the new hardware's bases are at least as large as the old. But if the piece of furniture is very valuable or an antique, or if the hardware is very attractive, the old hardware should not be removed. In this case, missing parts should be replaced with matching or similar hardware; a slight difference in design usually doesn't look bad.

Hardware stores, home centers, and similar stores offer a fair selection of furniture hardware; specialty hardware outlets and craft suppliers are usually better sources. The suppliers listed above for veneer woods also stock special hardware pieces.

Drawer Pulls and Handles. To tighten a loosely attached drawer pull, remove the pull and replace the screw with a longer one. If the screw is part of the pull, you'll have to make the hole in the wood smaller. When the hole is only slightly enlarged, you can tighten the pull by using a hollow fiber plug with the screw; for metal pulls, fit a piece of solid-core solder into the hole and then replace the screw. When the hole is much too big, insert wood toothpicks or thin shavings of wood, with glue applied on the outside, into the hole; let the glue dry and carefully trim them flush with the wood surface. Then dip the pull's screw into glue, replace the pull, and tighten the screw firmly. For a more substantial repair, enlarge the hole, glue a piece of dowel into it, and drill a new screw hole.

Hinges. Hinges that don't work properly usually have bent hinge pins; in this case, replace the hinges. If the hinges are loose, try using slightly longer screws to attach them. When the screw holes are very much enlarged, adjust them by one of the methods detailed above. If the hinge leaves are damaged and the hinges cannot be replaced, glue the hinges into position with epoxy or a rubber- or silicone-base adhesive.

Locks. Locks on old pieces are often damaged, and keys are often missing. If the piece of furniture is an antique, or the lock is very unusual, have it repaired by a professional. Otherwise, remove the damaged lock and take it to a locksmith; order a matching or similar lock to replace it.

Loose Metal Bands and Escutcheons. Old bands and escutcheons often have an attractive design and patina; don't replace them unless they're badly damaged. To secure a loose band or escutcheon, squeeze adhesive caulking compound under the metal, and press it down to bond it to the wood. If this doesn't work, fasten the band or escutcheon with tiny metal screws, of the same metal as the hardware. You must match the metals—brass to brass, copper to copper, steel to steel, or whatever. If you don't match the screws to the metal plate, the metal will corrode. Use several screws, placing them to form a pattern; drill pilot holes before inserting them.

Coverup Hardware. If old hardware holes are impossible to repair, or if you want to change the look of a piece entirely, the surface can be covered with new wood or metal escutcheon plates. Escutcheons are used particularly under drawer pulls or handles; many handles are made with escutcheon-type backers. Attach the escutcheons with adhesive or screws, matched metal to metal. If you're using escutcheon-type handles, no other treatment is necessary. If you're using an escutcheon under other hardware, drill new mounting holes as required. Keep your design simple, and try to match the style of the piece.

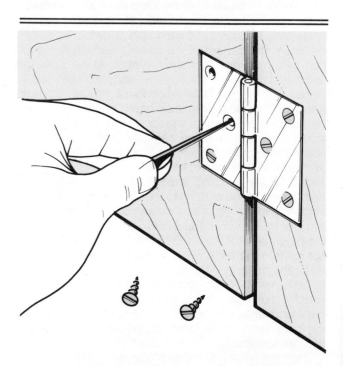

Enlarged screw holes can be made smaller with wood toothpicks, glued in and trimmed flush with the surface.

Chapter 10
Structural Repairs

Furniture that's had a lot of use very often has structural problems—loose or broken parts, wobbly legs, doors or drawers that don't work right. When you're refinishing an old piece, structural problems may be even more obvious after you've removed the finish; paint and varnish can hide defects, and stripping can cause damage. For these reasons, and because it's easier to work when you don't have to worry about hurting the finish, it's best to repair furniture after stripping and before preparing it for refinishing.

Like preparation and refinishing, repairs should be made in logical order. Depending on how much work a piece of furniture needs, the procedure may vary, but the basic order is always the same: first repair all joints and replace missing wood; then refinish the piece. Support or webbing repairs should be made before refinishing, upholstery repairs after refinishing is complete.

If parts are missing or support is inadequate, you'll probably need wood to match the piece of furniture. This can be a problem. Pine and oak are sold at most lumberyards and at home centers, but other furniture woods—walnut, cherry, mahogany, and other hardwoods—are harder to come by. Woodworking and millwork outlets usually stock and sell a variety of hardwoods, or can tell you where to find them. If you're looking for rare woods, the sources listed in Chapter 9 for veneers may be able to help you. And don't overlook auctions, used furniture outlets, and wrecking contractors; you may be able to pick up some real bargains in wood or old furniture.

Whenever possible, repairs should be made with the same wood used in the piece of furniture. If you can't find the wood you need, use a light-colored wood—maple, gum, birch, or even pine. It's always easier to stain a light repair area than to refinish an entire piece of furniture to match one part or patch. You may also be able to borrow a piece of wood from a hidden part of the piece—a drawer bottom, a back leg, or any inconspicuous part. In this case, use the new wood to replace the borrowed wood.

HOW FURNITURE IS MADE

All furniture is put together in a series of joints, and structural problems often involve joint weakening or failure. Some joints are simple, some complicated; some types are stronger than others. The joints used in good furniture are usually stronger than those in cheap pieces, but age and abuse can take their toll even when the original construction was good. To prevent more serious damage, all joints should be repaired as soon as possible when they loosen or separate.

Very old furniture is usually put together with mortise-and-tenon joints, which consist of a prong held in a hole. The dovetail joint is used in good-quality furniture; butt and lapped joints, the weakest types, are also the easiest to make, and are often used in cheap pieces. Other joints used in furniture manufacturing include blank or stopped mortise-and-tenon joints, dadoes and stopped or dovetailed dadoes, miters, and doweled, rabbeted, or splined joints. Each type of joint has specific uses and applications.

Mortise-and-Tenon Joints. In this type of joint, a prong or tongue of wood—the tenon—is secured in a hole—the mortise—in the joining piece. If the joint is blank or stopped, the mortise doesn't extend completely through the joining piece, and the end of the tenon is not visible on the outside of the joint. Mortise-and-tenon joints are extremely strong; they're used chiefly in chairs and tables.

Dovetail Joints. Dovetail joints consist of wedge-shaped openings, the dovetails, holding matching pins cut in the joining piece. These joints are the pride of cabinetmakers, in both old and new furniture. The through dovetail is the early version; in this joint, the dovetail goes completely through both pieces of wood. The pins in handmade dovetails are usually narrower than the spaces between the pins. On a real antique piece, only a few dovetails are used, and the tails and pins don't match exactly; with modern equipment, the tails and the pins are exactly the same size, and more dovetails are used in each joint. Some dovetail joints are blind; the pins don't extend completely through the joining piece, and only the top or face of the joint is visible.

Dado Joints. A dado is a slot cut into the face or end of a piece of wood; the joining piece fits into this slot. In a simple dado joint, the slot goes completely across the wood, and the edges of the joining piece are visible along the edges of the base piece. In a stopped or blind dado, the joint does not extend completely across the face of the wood, and is not visible from the edges.

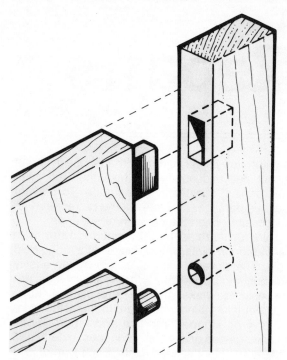

The mortise-and-tenon joint, used chiefly in chair and table frames, is very strong. Both square and round tenons are used in furniture construction.

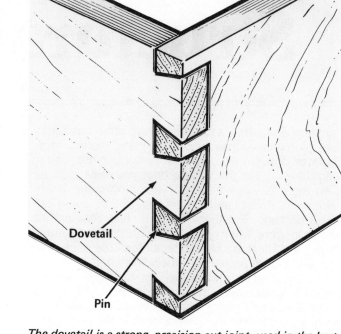

Dovetail

Pin

The dovetail is a strong, precision-cut joint, used in the best furniture. On antiques, dovetails were hand-cut; these are less even than machine-cut joints.

Dadoes and stopped dadoes have considerable shear strength, and are used chiefly for shelving. The dovetail dado is a dado with a slight dovetail at the bottom; it's a fancy cabinet joint, strong and especially good-looking. In very old furniture, a dovetail dado joint is a real work of art because of the time the cabinetmaker had to spend to cut it.

Butt Joints. In this type of joint, the joining pieces are simply butted together—face to face, edge to edge, or face to edge—with no integral fastener. Butt joints are weak, and are sometimes fastened or held together with metal surface plates. Wood or metal butt joints held with a metal fastener such as a nail, screw, or mending plate, or a specially machined metal or plastic

Dado   Stopped Dado   Dovetail Dado

In the dado joint (left), used chiefly for shelving, a slot or groove is cut into one piece to hold the end of the joining piece. The groove of a stopped or blind dado (center) does not extend completely across the wood. The dovetail dado (right) is cut with a dovetail at the bottom for extra strength.

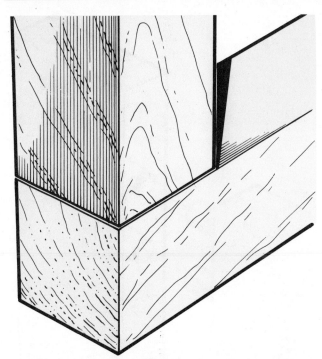

In the butt joint, the two joining pieces are simply butted together. Nails, screws, or metal mending plates are sometimes used for reinforcements.

are used to join the ends of long pieces. Lapped joints offer a large glue area, but they aren't particularly strong; they're often used in drawer guide framing pieces, and may be pinned with nails or screws from the back. To strengthen lap joints, some cabinetmakers cut them with a dovetail configuration.

Miter Joints. In a miter, the joining pieces are cut at a 45-degree angle and joined to form a right angle. Miters are used for decorative molding and for frames; they are very weak, and are often reinforced with dowels, splines, or mechanical fasteners. Many cabinet-type pieces have mitered corner joints, almost always reinforced by dowels or by a plywood spline running the length of each joint. In less expensive furniture, miter joints may be supported with a strip of wood nailed or screwed to the inside corner of the joint. Sometimes triangular glue blocks are used for strength; the blocks may be reinforced by screws.

Doweled Joints. The doweled joint is a simple variation of the mortise-and-tenon joint, with dowels instead of a cut tenon holding the joining pieces together. Doweled joints require precision equipment. They are strong, and are common in chairs, tables, and cabinets, usually on stretchers and other framing pieces.

Rabbet Joints. The rabbet is a reinforced butt joint, with one or both joining members notched to fit together; it is usually reinforced with screws or nails. Rabbet joints are easy to make and very strong; they are used chiefly for shelving and at the corners of cabinet pieces. A stopped rabbet extends only partway through the wood. Rabbet joints are sometimes made with a dado variation.

fitting, are called mechanical joints; they are used in chairs, tables, dressers, and cabinet pieces.

Lapped Joints. Lapped joints—cross-laps, half-laps, and sloped laps—are cut with both joining pieces notched or slanted to the same depth. Cross-laps are used to join crossing pieces; half-laps and sloped laps

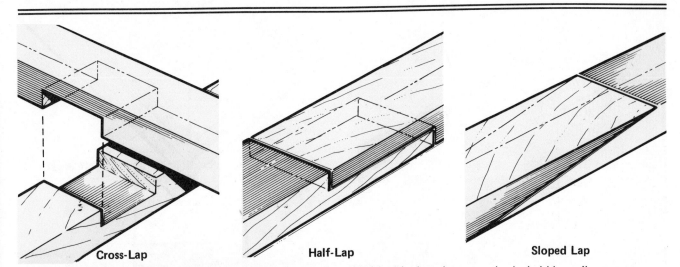

| Cross-Lap | Half-Lap | Sloped Lap |

In lapped joints, the joining pieces are cut to the same depth and held with glue; they may also be held by nails or screws. The cross-lap (left) joins crossing pieces; half-laps (center) and sloped laps (right) join the ends of long pieces. Some lapped joints are cut with a dovetail for additional strength.

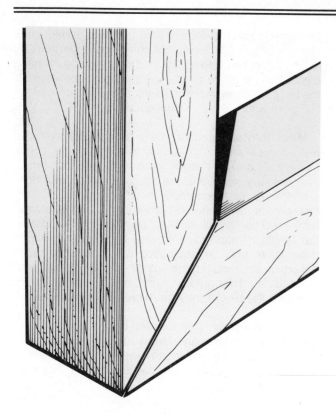

The miter joint, used for frames and molding, consists of two pieces cut at a 45-degree angle, joined at a right angle.

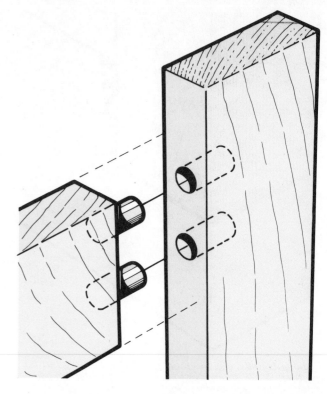

The doweled joint is a variation of the mortise-and-tenon, with dowels instead of a tenon holding the pieces together.

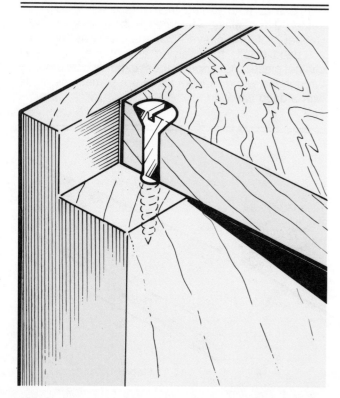

In the rabbet joint, one or both joining members are notched. Screws or nails are usually used for reinforcement.

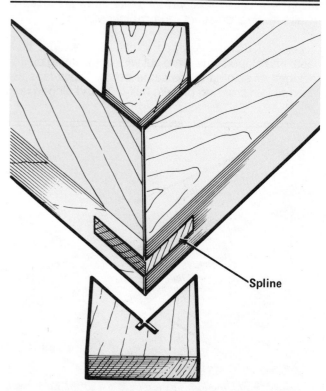

Spline

The splined joint is held together by a reinforcing spline, fitted into matching grooves in the joining members.

Splined Joints. In a splined joint, the edges of the joining pieces are grooved or dadoed to match each other, and a reinforcing spline—usually plywood or hardboard—is inserted into the grooves or dadoes to hold the pieces together. Splined joints are used chiefly to join narrow boards; in modern construction, plywood is often used to eliminate the need for these joints.

BASIC REPAIR TECHNIQUES

Structural problems in furniture can be defined in terms of three things: the material itself, the way it's put together, and the way it functions. The material itself is the problem when a part is broken, warped, or missing; the way it's put together is involved when joints fail or parts aren't fitted properly. The way a piece of furniture functions depends on both material and construction, and functional problems can always be traced to one or both of these sources. Nothing can turn an all-around loser into a quality piece of furniture, but with a few basic repair techniques, you can handle most structural furniture problems.

Rebuilding Loose Joints

When a joint fails, you have two problems to deal with: the immediate functional problem and the long-term effect of the failure on the rest of the frame. A loose joint that's not repaired today may not break tomorrow, but it will put stress on other joints—and in a week's time, one wobbly leg may become two. To prevent simple structural problems from turning into more serious ones, loose or separated joints should be repaired immediately.

Gluing. The simplest solution is usually the best one, in repairs as well as in refinishing. When you discover a loose joint, first make sure the screws (if any) are tight; then try to repair it with an adhesive—plastic resin, epoxy, or resorcinol. Force the adhesive into the loose joint with a glue injector; if you can, wiggle the joint to distribute the adhesive. Clamp the joint for about two days, until the adhesive is completely cured. If possible, strengthen the glued joint with a glue block, as detailed below.

After gluing the loose joint, put the piece of furniture back into service. Check the joint again in a few weeks. If it has worked loose again, it can't be permanently repaired by regluing; you'll have to reinforce it, resecure it, or rebuild it completely.

Reinforcing: Glue Blocks and Steel Braces. Glue blocks, the original furniture braces, are solid pieces of wood used to reinforce corner joints and provide additional support. Steel corner plates and angle braces perform the same function, but they can detract from the appearance of the piece of furniture, and they can also lower its value. For this reason, glue blocks are

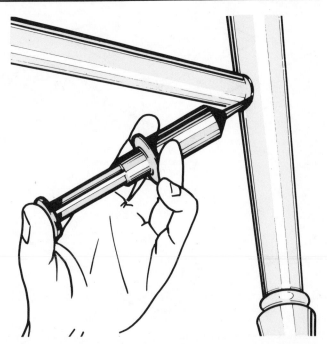

In many cases, a loose joint can simply be reglued. Force glue into the joint with a glue injector, and clamp the piece firmly until the adhesive is completely cured.

still an important part of furniture repairs. Valuable pieces of furniture, antiques, and good reproductions should always be repaired with glue blocks instead of steel braces when possible.

Glue blocks for corner braces can be either square or triangular. Square blocks are used chiefly as outside support braces, or on long joints, such as the inside corners of drawers, where cutting a triangle would be impractical. In most cases, triangular glue blocks are preferable.

Glue blocks can be cut from any square stock, but hardwood is preferred. To make a glue block, cut a square piece of wood in half diagonally; the larger the piece of wood, the greater the gluing surface of the block. The length of the blocks will depend on the project; on the average, two inches is adequate. To strengthen chair and table legs, cut triangular braces from one-inch nominal boards, as large as necessary. At the right-angle corner of the block, cut off a diagonal or make a notch to fit around the leg. For braces, 1 × 2 lumber works well.

To install a triangular glue block, spread adhesive on the two right-angle sides or edges. Set the block into the corner and twist it slightly to distribute the adhesive on the bonding surfaces. Small glue blocks can be strengthened by nails driven through the block into the furniture frame; drill pilot holes for the nails to make sure you don't split the wood. To strengthen chair and table braces, drive three screws through the block and into the frame, one screw straight into the corner and

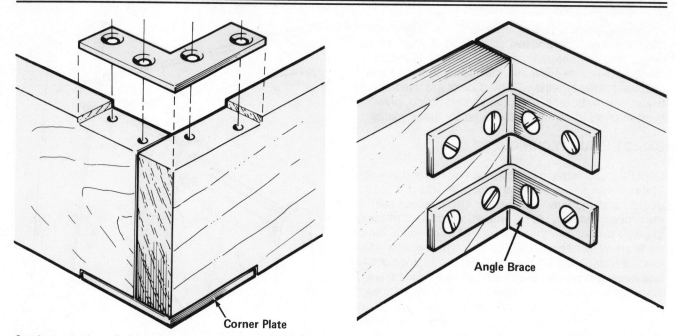

Steel corner plates (left) and angle braces (right) are often used to reinforce weak joints, especially in inexpensive furniture. Because they can detract from the appearance of the piece, and can also lower its value, they should never be used on valuable or antique furniture.

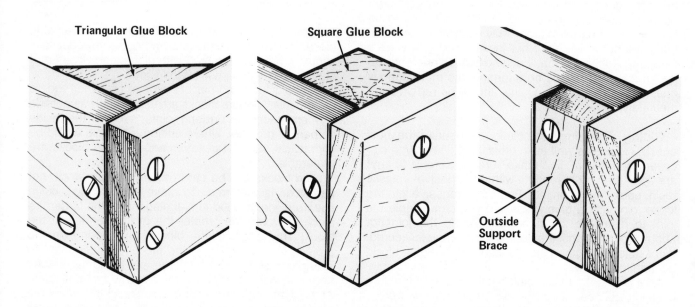

Glue blocks, the original furniture braces, are used to reinforce corner joints and provide additional support. Triangular glue blocks (left) are usually preferable for corner braces. Square glue blocks are used on long joints where cutting a triangle would be impractical (center), and as outside support braces (right). If possible, glue blocks should be cut from hardwood.

one straight into each side, at an angle to the inside block edge. Predrill the screw holes for the block in both the block and the frame.

Sometimes a corner joint is held by a steel bracket instead of a glue block. If the leg wobbles, first make sure the nut that holds the bracket is securely tightened. If this doesn't solve the problem, and the bracket is set into notches in the frame, it may not be seated properly. Remove the nut and reseat the bracket; then replace the nut securely.

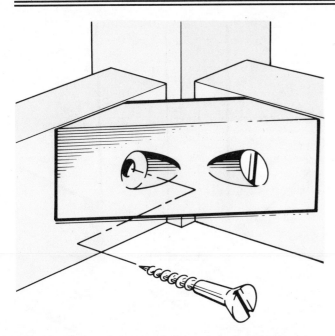

To strengthen a chair or table leg, cut a triangular brace, and cut off one corner to fit across the leg. Attach the block with glue and two or, if possible, three screws.

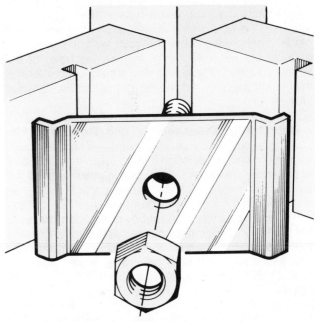

Some corner joints are held by steel brackets, set into notches in the frame. If a bracketed leg wobbles, tighten the bracket nut; if necessary, reseat the bracket.

Resecuring: Screws and Glue. If a loose joint would be difficult to take apart, you may be able to solve the problem with a long screw. First, align the joint and drill a pilot hole for the screw. Then enlarge the top of the pilot hole so that a small piece of dowel can be installed over the screw head, as illustrated. Coat the screw with glue and drive it into the joint so that it pulls the joint tightly together. Before you tighten the screw, try to force adhesive into the loose joint; this will help strengthen the joint. Then tighten the screw firmly.

To cover the screw head, cut a piece of dowel to fit the enlarged hole; it should be slightly longer than the opening, so that the end of the dowel will protrude slightly above the surface of the frame. Insert the dowel plug with glue, making sure the end of the dowel is flush with the head of the screw, and let the glue dry completely; then carefully cut the end of the dowel flush with the surface and sand it smooth. You'll probably have to refinish the frame so the dowel matches, and you may want to install false dowel plugs at the other joints in the frame so that they match. The dowel will give the frame a hand-made pinned or pegged look.

The screw/plug trick can also be used to repair loose rungs and backs, but the pieces involved must be large enough to accept the screw and dowel. Small parts such as turnings and slats may split when a screw is driven into them.

For the strongest screw-reinforced joint, the screw should be driven into a piece of dowel instead of the frame itself. This isn't always possible, but if you can,

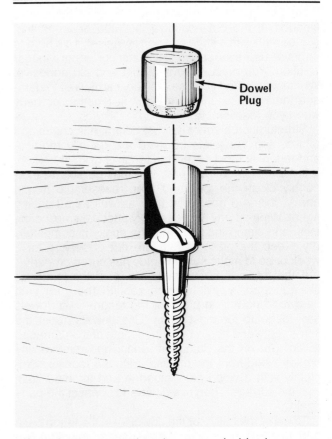

Dowel Plug

A loose joint can sometimes be resecured with a long screw, coated with glue and driven into the joint. Cover the screw head with a dowel plug, and refinish the frame.

disassemble the joint, drill a hole at the screw point, and plug the hole with a dowel, gluing the dowel into place. Then reassemble the joint with a screw and glue, as above. If you want to hide the head of the screw, enlarge the hole for a dowel plug; or countersink the screw slightly and fill the depression with wood filler.

Rebuilding: Disassembly and Doweling. Rebuilding a joint—or a series of joints—is not as tough as it might sound, although it does require a good deal of patience. You must work slowly to make sure all the parts are in the right places and all parts fit tightly. To disassemble the joint, pull it carefully apart. If it doesn't come apart easily, use a rubber or wooden mallet to tap the frame pieces apart, but be careful not to damage the wood. Don't overlook the possibility that the joint was assembled with nails or screws as well as adhesive; in this case, you should remove the fasteners before you break the adhesive. If you can't remove them, break the adhesive bond and pry the joint apart very carefully. Don't force the joint apart; if the nails or screws are embedded too firmly, you'll split or splinter the wood. If prying would damage the wood, consider sawing the joint apart. Use a hacksaw with a thin blade that will go through metal and not leave a wide cut.

After the joint is disassembled, it must be thoroughly cleaned. If the old adhesive is brittle or crumbling, scrape it off with a knife or a narrow chisel; if it's hard to remove, use sandpaper, hot water, or a hot vinegar solution. You must remove all dirt and old adhesive. Whatever method you use, be very careful not to damage the wood, or the joint won't fit together properly when you reassemble it.

Structural problems are most common in chairs and tables, and the joints involved are usually mortise-and-tenon. In most cases, the tenon is worn or broken. If the damage isn't too bad, you may be able to thoroughly clean the joint and then reassemble it with epoxy; this is a good joint filler as well as a bonding agent. Wipe off any excess epoxy after assembling the joint, and clamp the joint until the epoxy is completely dry. Keep the piece of furniture out of service for a week or so to make sure the glue has cured properly.

If the tenon is badly damaged, or if the joint was sawed apart, you'll have to rebuild the joint with hardwood dowels in place of the tenon—two dowels are adequate for most joints. Use dowels about the same width and about twice the length of the damaged tenon. Cut off the damaged tenon, and remove any broken wood from the mortise. Plug the mortise completely with a wood plug, glued in and trimmed flush with the surface. Then use dowels to connect the parts again.

To make the holes for the dowels—in the tenon base and in the plugged mortise—use a doweling jig, clamped to the edge of the wood and adjusted to center the dowel holes. Dowel center points can also be

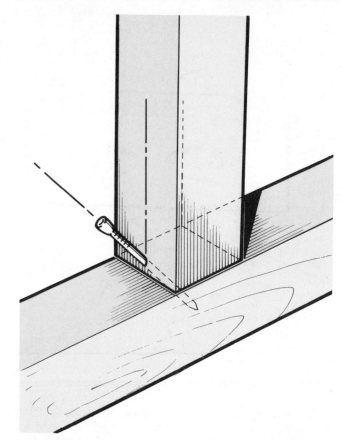

If a joint doesn't come apart easily, it may be held by nails or screws; these fasteners should be removed before the joint is disassembled.

used, but they aren't as accurate as a jig. Drill the holes to a total depth of about ¼ inch deeper than the length of the dowel, to allow for glue buildup under the dowels.

Score the sides of the dowels with pliers and round the ends slightly with sandpaper or a file. This improves glue distribution, and makes insertion easier and more accurate. Apply glue to the dowels and insert them into the holes in one side of the joint; then coat the edge of the wood with glue and slip the other joint piece onto the dowels. Tap the joint together with a rubber or wooden mallet, wipe off any glue that oozes out of the joint, and clamp the joint firmly for about two days, until the glue is completely set.

COMMON STRUCTURAL PROBLEMS

The basic joint repair techniques can be applied to all types of furniture, but each kind of frame has its own individual structural problems. Chairs are prone to broken rungs and split seats; tabletops warp; drawers stick or tip; caning and upholstery wear out. With common sense and a few particulars, you can keep all your furniture in good repair.

Chairs

Loose Joints. Seat frames are held by mortise-and tenon or doweled joints supported by triangular glue blocks, notched to fit the legs. If you catch a loose joint in time, repair it with glue. If the joint is broken, you'll have to disassemble it and replace the dowels, as detailed above. The triangular glue blocks will probably be glued and screwed to the frame, and the dowel joint might even be supported with hidden nail or screw fasteners. Separate the joint carefully with an old screwdriver or a stiff-bladed putty knife; then replace the dowels. Make sure the joint is clean and dry before you reassemble it.

Sometimes you can use a mechanical fastener—an angle brace or a chair leg brace—to mend the frame. This, of course, really depends on the value of the furniture; do not lower the value of an antique with a piece of metal. Metal reinforcements are useless unless the joint is tightly fitted together, but they can be used to make a firm joint even tighter. Fasten the braces with brass screws, and make sure the screws are long enough.

Fasten the metal angle to one side of the chair frame; predrill the screw holes. Insert a piece of thin cardboard under the opposite part of the angle; then drill the screw holes for that side. Drive in the screws fairly tight, remove the cardboard, and finish tightening the screws; when the screws are final-tightened, the angle will pull the joint tightly together to bridge the gap left by the cardboard.

Back Rails, Spindles, and Slats. On chairs with horizontal rails across the back, the rails are mortised into the side posts; on chairs with vertical spindles or slats, these parts are mortised into a curved or straight top rail. Rails, spindles, and slats can all be replaced easily, but replacement may be fairly expensive—don't bother if the chair isn't worth the investment. To replace a broken or missing part, have a millwork or woodworking shop custom-make a new part.

First, disassemble the chair back; it will probably be joined at the legs, seat, and rail. Carefully pry the joints apart, removing any nails or screws. Disassemble only the joints involved in the repair; it usually isn't necessary to completely disassemble the piece to get at the part. If you aren't sure you'll be able to reassemble the chair back, number the parts as you take them out.

Take the broken part, and a similar undamaged part, to the millwork or woodworking shop for duplication. When you have the new part, carefully clean the old adhesive from the joints. Then reassemble the chair with the new part, gluing each joint. Clamp the chair with strap clamps until the adhesive dries, and then refinish the chair completely.

Outdoor chairs made with wooden slats can be repaired the same way, but the slats can usually be replaced with wide moldings or thin boards. To replace a

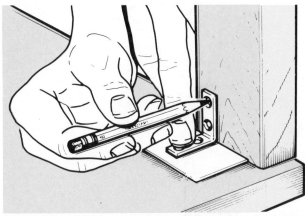

Insert a piece of thin cardboard under one side of an angle brace; remove the cardboard before final-tightening the screws on that side. This pulls the joint together.

broken slat, cut and shape a piece of wide molding or a board to fit the frame. If the slats are fastened with screws, drill screw holes in the new slat and attach it with the old screws or matching new ones. If they're fastened with rivets, drill the old rivets out, and replace them with self-tapping or panhead sheet metal screws.

Loose Legs, Rungs, and Spindles. Loose rungs or spindles—and, where no bracing is used, loose legs—can sometimes be mended by forcing glue into the joints, but a part mended this way may work loose again. For a more permanent repair, carefully separate the part from the frame; if both ends are loose, remove the entire piece. For very stubborn joints, twist the part slightly to break the glue bond; if necessary, use self-locking pliers. Pad the part to prevent damage to the wood from the pliers.

Remove the old adhesive completely from the part and from its socket; glue does not bond well to old glue. Be careful not to remove any wood from the end of the part, or it won't fit right. After removing the old glue, test each end of the part in its socket. If the ends fit snugly, apply glue to the socket and reinsert the loose part. Clamp the reglued joint and let it dry completely.

If the part is loose in its socket, you'll have to enlarge it to make a firm joint; if the tenon end is cracked, you'll have to reinforce it. Apply a thin coat of glue to the tenon, and wrap it tightly with silk thread; if necessary, apply more glue and cover the tenon with another layer of thread. Let the threaded tenon dry for a day and then glue the reinforced end firmly into the socket; insert it carefully so you don't disturb the thread. Clamp the joint and let it dry completely.

Very loose legs or rungs can be wedged to fit if the tenon is sound. Clamp the part in a vise or have a helper hold it; then saw very carefully into the center of the tenon end, as illustrated. The cut must be square and centered, roughly the depth of the part that fits into

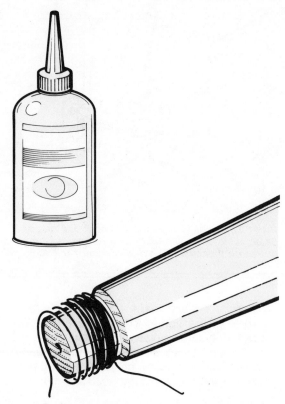

the socket—about ¾ inch. For small parts, use a hacksaw or a coping saw to make the cut; for thicker parts, use a backsaw or combination saw.

From a piece of soft wood—pine quarter-round, if you have it—cut a thin wedge to fit the width and depth of the saw cut in the tenon. The object here is to spread the saw cut slightly with the wedge, thus enlarging the tenon to fit the socket. When you're satisfied that the wedge is the right size, very carefully tap the wedge into the saw cut. When the tenon is slightly enlarged, stop pounding and trim off any excess wood from the wedge with a utility knife or pocketknife. Be careful not to pound the wedge too far; excessive wedging will split the tenon. To test the wedge, insert the end of it into the saw cut and tap it down with a screwdriver handle. If you see the wood on both sides of the cut start to spread, the wedge is too wide. Finally, apply glue and reassemble the joint as above.

You may not be able to disassemble the piece of furniture for this wedging procedure. In this case, there are two more ways to do the job. If the joint is extremely loose, and appearance is not important, remove as much adhesive as you can. Make several thin wedges from molding—pine lattice is a good selection. Dip the ends of the wedges in adhesive and drive the wedges with a hammer around the loose part, between the part and the socket. Then, with a utility knife, trim the ends of the wedges flush with the surrounding wood surface. Equalize the pressure from the wedges as you drive

If the tenon is cracked or loose, coat it with glue and wrap it with silk thread. Let the glue dry; then glue the tenon back into its socket.

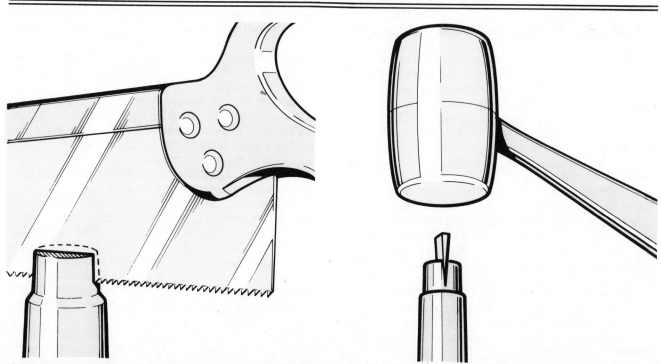

If the tenon is very loose, enlarge it with a small wedge. Saw straight into the tenon (left), and cut a thin wedge to fit the saw cut. Tap the wedge carefully into the cut (right) to enlarge the tenon slightly; make sure you don't crack the tenon. Then trim off any excess wood and glue the enlarged tenon back into its socket.

them in; unless you place them carefully, the wedges can throw the part out of alignment, further weakening the joint.

Where appearance is more important, drill a 1/16-inch hole through the side of the joint and the loose part. Then make a metal pin from a 10d common or finishing nail. Cut off the head of the nail with a hacksaw; apply a drop or two of glue to the drilled hole and drive in the nail. Countersink the pin with a nail set or another 10d nail, and fill the hole with wood filler.

Broken Rungs and Spindles. Splits and breaks in nonstructural rungs and spindles can be repaired with glue. Separate the broken ends of the part and apply glue to each piece; or, if the part is only cracked, force glue into the crack with a glue injector. Join the pieces carefully, pressing them firmly together, and remove any excess glue. Wrap a piece of wax paper around the part, and then wrap the mended break firmly with a piece of cord, to keep the part aligned properly. Clamp the chair firmly with a strap clamp or a rope, and let the glue dry completely.

Broken Arms, Legs, and Other Structural Parts. Where strength is important, the broken part must be reinforced. The best reinforcement is a dowel pinning the broken pieces together. Use 1/8-inch to 3/8-inch dowel, depending on how thick the broken part is; drill the dowel holes with a bit of the same size.

Where appearance matters, drill through the side of the joint into the loose part. Pin the joint with a nail through the drilled hole.

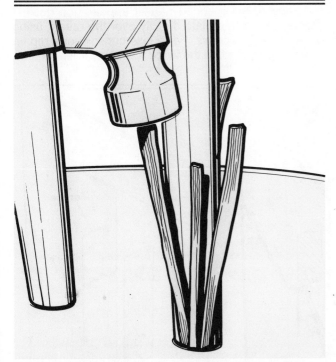

Extremely loose joints can be wedged from the outside. Dip thin wedges in glue and pound them in around the loose part; then trim them flush.

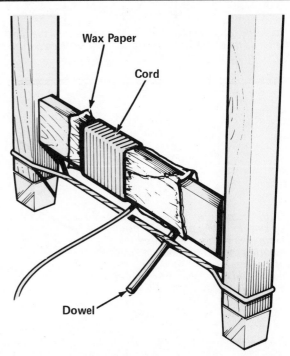

A split in a nonstructural part can be glued. Wrap a piece of wax paper around the glued part, bind it with cord, and clamp it firmly until the glue is dry.

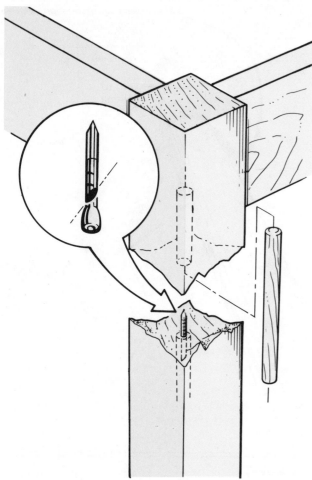

Separate the broken ends of the part. In the center of one end, and at a right angle to the break, drill a one-inch-deep hole, the same diameter as the dowel. This hole marks the dowel location. Cut off the head of a 16d nail and insert the nail in the hole, point out; the point of the nail should protrude only slightly above the broken surface. To mark the dowel location on the other piece of the broken part, match the pieces and press them firmly together; the point of the nail will leave a tiny hole in the matching piece. Then drill straight into the second piece, about one inch deep.

Measure the dowel holes, and cut a piece of dowel ¼ inch shorter than their total depth, to allow for glue buildup. Score the sides of the dowel with pliers and round the ends slightly with sandpaper or a file; this improves glue distribution and makes insertion easier. Apply glue to one end of the dowel and insert it into the hole in one end; then apply glue to the protruding dowel and to the face of the break, and push the other piece of the broken part onto the dowel. Match the parts perfectly, wipe off excess adhesive, and clamp the mended part as above.

Where doweling isn't possible, or where you want to provide extra strength, use a steel mending plate to reinforce the break. Mending plates can be used on any flat surface. Glue the break as above, and let it dry completely. Then add a mending plate, long enough to span the break and narrow enough to be inconspicuous; use a plate with screw holes beveled to accept flathead screws.

Place the mending plate on the inside or least obvious face of the mended part. If appearance doesn't matter, secure the plate directly over the break, using flathead brass screws. For a less conspicuous repair, mortise the plate into the wood. Carefully trace the out-

To mark the dowel location, drill into one end of the part and insert a nail with its head cut off. Press the ends firmly together to mark the drilling point.

For extra strength, reinforce the break with a steel mending plate. Mortise out the plate area with a sharp chisel (left), first scoring the outline and then cutting out the excess wood. When the mortise is smooth and level, glue the mending plate into place (right); predrill the screw holes.

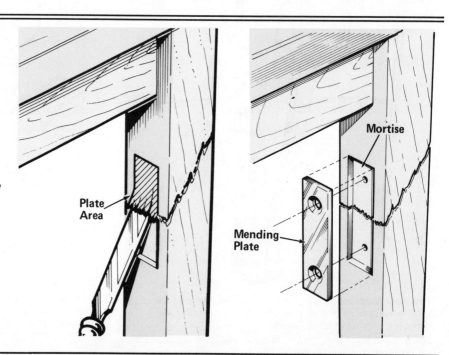

Plate Area

Mortise

Mending Plate

line of the mending plate onto the wood with a scratch awl or a sharp nail. Score the wood along the outline with a series of straight-down chisel cuts, as deep as you want the mortise—about ¼ inch for most plates, allowing space to cover the plate with wood filler. Cross-score the wood at right angles to the outline; then turn the chisel over, bevel side down, and remove the excess wood in the scored outline, working with the grain of the wood and removing only a little wood at a time.

When the bottom of the mortise is as smooth and level as you can make it, test the plate for fit, and make any adjustments necessary. When the plate fits exactly, drill pilot holes for the screws and coat the mortise with a thin layer of glue. Dip the screws in glue, position the plate in the mortise, and drive the screws firmly in. Let the glue dry for several days, and then cover the mending plate evenly with wood filler or a veneer patch; finish the filler to match the wood.

Split Seats. Split chair seats can be repaired with a series of ⅛-inch dowels along the break, and reinforced with metal mending plates. The seat must be completely removed for doweling.

Drill holes for the dowels in each side of the broken seat, about one inch deep (or as deep as possible) and spaced about four to six inches apart. Use a doweling jig, clamped to the broken seat, to drill the dowel holes; dowel center points can also be used, but they aren't as accurate. Cut and score each dowel as above, ¼ inch less than the total length of the dowel holes.

Apply glue to one end of each dowel, and insert the dowels into the holes along one side of the broken seat; then apply glue to the protruding dowel ends and to the broken edge, and join the two parts. Tap the pieces of the seat together with a rubber or wooden mallet, and wipe off any excess glue. Lightly clamp the glued seat, and let it dry for at least two days. For extra strength, you can add metal mending plates to span the break, as above—four plates should be adequate. Finally, reassemble the chair.

Insert Chair Seats. Chair seats set in or on frames are usually boards or plywood, covered with padding and cloth. These seats seldom split, but when they do, the simplest solution is to replace the seat with a new piece of plywood—⅜-inch thickness is best. If ⅜-inch plywood won't fit properly after the padding has been added, you may have to use ¼-inch plywood, but anything less than this will not provide the needed support. Use the old chair seat as a template or pattern to cut out the new one.

Padded chair seats are usually held to the frame with screws driven through glue blocks. Look carefully for these screws; the cloth covering the padding may hide them. Remove all fasteners, and replace them the same way to hold the new chair seat.

If the upholstery on insert seats is worn or damaged,

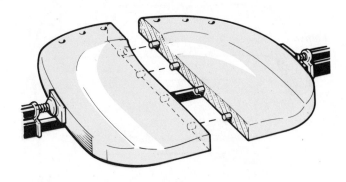

Repair a split chair seat with a series of 1/8-inch dowels, glued about 4 inches apart along the split. Clamp the seat firmly until the glue is completely cured.

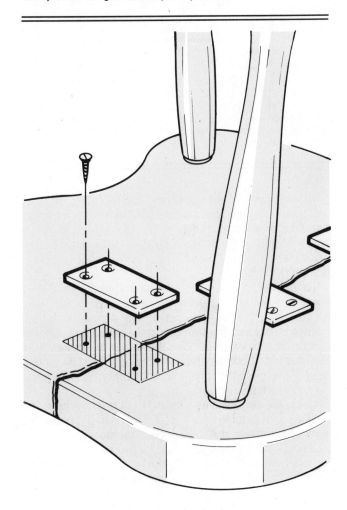

For a stronger repair, dowel the seat together; then reinforce the doweled seat with metal mending plates set across the break. Finally, reassemble the chair.

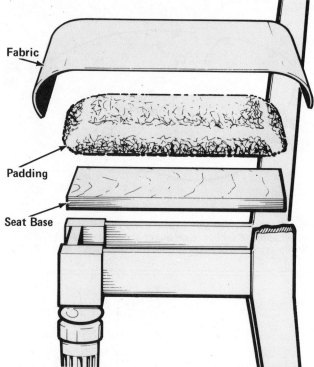

Fabric

Padding

Seat Base

Insert seats consist of a board or plywood seat base covered with padding and then fabric. The seat rests in or on the chair frame, and is usually secured with screws.

it can easily be replaced. Dining room chairs are usually padded with cotton batting; some chairs have foam padding or a combination of foam and cotton. Both types of padding are available precut for chair seats. For most chairs, the padding should be about ¾ inch to one inch thick.

To recover an insert chair seat, remove the seat from the chair. The seat is usually a piece of plywood, held to the chair frame by screws; the screws may be counterbored into the frame or may go up through the corner glue blocks. Remove the tacks or staples that hold the old upholstery fabric to the seat, and lift off the fabric. Refinish the chair, if necessary, before proceeding further.

Using the old fabric as a pattern, cut the new fabric to fit. If the old padding on the chair seat is in good shape, it can be reused; if it's damaged, replace it with new padding. You may be able to fluff and smooth old cotton padding; if it's badly flattened, add a layer of foam padding to build the seat cushion up to ¾ to one inch.

Lay the new fabric flat, wrong side up, and center the padded seat on it upside down. Fold the edges of the fabric up over the seat, stretching it firmly onto the plywood; if desired, tape the fabric firmly down with masking tape. Starting at the center of one side, fold the fabric under and attach it to the seat with heavy-duty staples in a staple gun. If the new fabric is very

heavy, flatheaded upholstery tacks may be more secure. Set staples or tacks one to 1½ inches apart along the side of the seat.

When the first side is completely attached, restretch the fabric; then staple or tack the opposite side. Turn the seat over and smooth the padding; be sure the fabric is straight, with no wrinkles. Then turn the seat over again and fasten the other two sides. At the corners, fold the fabric in to miter it neatly; if necessary, staple or tack each layer separately. Finally, staple a scrap piece of the new fabric to the seat, in case repairs are necessary in the future.

Replace the chair seat in the frame, and resecure it. Replace all the screws and tighten them firmly.

Legs and Feet

The legs and feet of furniture pieces—especially heavy cabinets, dressers, and bookcases—are subjected to both weight and, when they're moved, lateral stress. Pushing a heavily loaded piece of furniture can cause problems even if it doesn't cause immediate breakage, and these problems are very common in old pieces. Structural breaks should be repaired as above.

Loose Casters. A caster is secured by a metal rod, driven into a hole drilled in the bottom of the leg. When the piece of furniture is moved, stress on the caster rod can damage the wood around it, enlarging the hole and loosening the caster. If the damage isn't too bad, the casters may be loose; if it's been ignored long enough, the casters may fall out when the piece is lifted, or the ends of the legs may be split. Both problems can be solved.

To tighten loose casters, use metal or plastic caster sleeve inserts, available in several sizes. Remove the loose caster and tap the insert into the hole in the leg; no adhesive is needed. The sleeve should fit snugly; if it doesn't, use larger inserts. Insert the caster into the sleeve; this should solve the problem.

If the leg is split, remove all the casters on the piece. Apply glue along the split, and press the glued edges firmly together; wipe off any excess. To reinforce the break, bind the split with several wraps of fine black steel wire. On many pieces of furniture, there is a ridge or a crevice at the caster point; if you wrap the wire around the leg at this point, the repair will not be obvious. If the leg doesn't have any carving or decoration at this point, you can notch the wood all the way around with a triangular file, and then wrap the wire in the notch. Treat all legs the same way so that they match.

One Leg Shorter Than the Rest. When this happens, you may be tempted to cut the other legs down to match the shorter one, but don't do it—instead, build up the short leg to match the others. Cutting usually results in serious mismatching, besides shortening the piece and ruining its design.

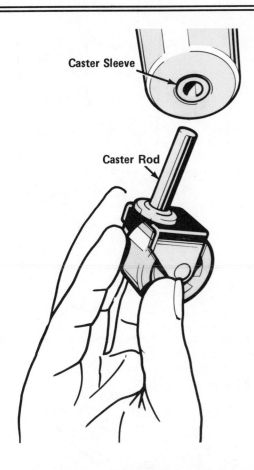

Caster Sleeve

Caster Rod

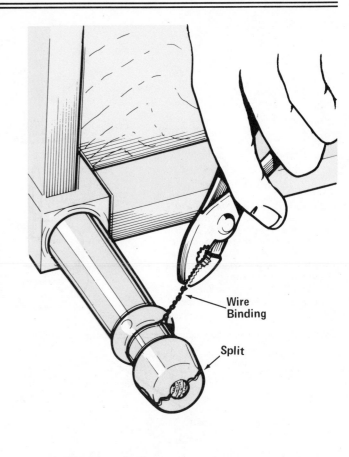

Wire Binding

Split

A caster is held in place by a metal rod set into the leg. When the caster hole is enlarged by stress on the rod, tap a caster sleeve into the hole and insert the rod into the sleeve (left). When the leg is split, remove the caster completely (right); glue the split together, and bind the leg with wire to reinforce the break. Then bind the other legs to match.

If the leg is only a little too short, use a metal leg cap to build it up. These caps, made in several sizes, have from one to three prongs on a metal base. To install a cap, just hammer in the prongs. To make sure you don't split the wood, center the cap on the leg and lightly tap it to mark the prong positions; then drill tiny holes to accept the prongs.

If a metal cap doesn't work, you may be able to add a wood extender to the leg. Cut the extender from the same wood as the piece of furniture, if possible; shape it to match. Fit the extender exactly and then glue and nail it to the bottom of the short leg; countersink the nails. You'll probably have to refinish the entire piece to blend the extender with the rest of the wood.

If the gap is really wide, you can V-notch the leg and the extender and glue the parts together, forming an A-shaped brace. This is a very strong repair, and will give the piece a real hand-made look, so you don't have to match the wood exactly. Assemble the joint with glue and countersunk small nails; drive the nails where they won't show, and fill the holes with wood filler. Even if the holes are visible, it won't look bad.

Doors and Other Flat Parts

Splits. Split doors, panels, cabinet backs, and other flat parts should be repaired with glue and, if possible, with dowels, as detailed above. Very thin door panels and cabinet backs cannot be repaired, and should be replaced. Where appearance is not important, as on the back of a door that's always left closed, metal mending plates can be used for reinforcement.

Sagging or Binding Doors. Sagging is usually caused by faulty hinge operation; make sure the hinges are working properly, as detailed in Chapter 9, "Surface Repairs." Binding can be caused by faulty hinges or by excess humidity. Swelling from humidity or moisture vapor is most common in spring and summer, and is most likely to affect wood that hasn't been properly sealed; in fall and winter, when the humidity is lower, the wood will shrink again.

Before you work on the wood, adjust the hinges. If the door binds at the top on the latch side, the top hinge is probably loose; tighten the screws, as detailed in

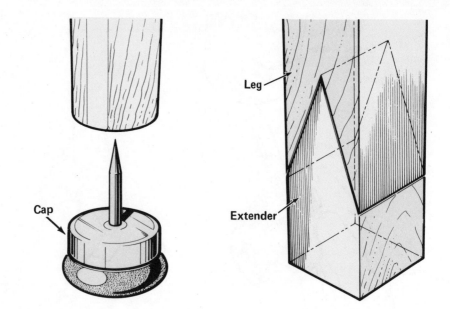

Leg

Cap

Extender

If the leg is only a little too short, use a metal cap to build it up (left). Center the cap on the leg; predrill starter holes so the prongs don't split the wood. If the leg is much too short, cut a V-shaped extender piece from matching wood (right). Fit the leg and the extender together, and nail and glue them firmly.

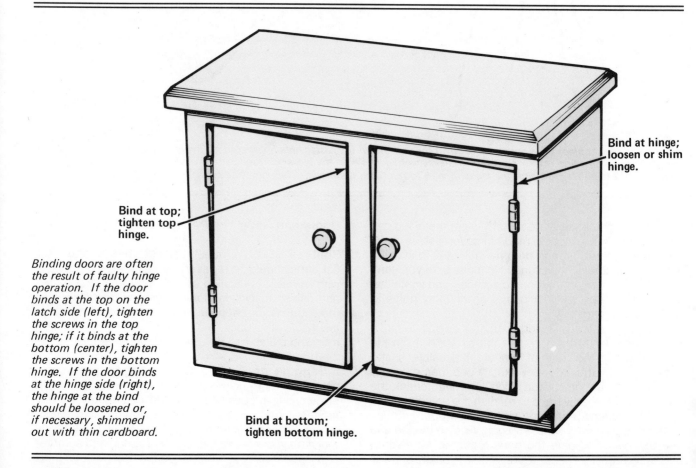

Bind at hinge; loosen or shim hinge.

Bind at top; tighten top hinge.

Binding doors are often the result of faulty hinge operation. If the door binds at the top on the latch side (left), tighten the screws in the top hinge; if it binds at the bottom (center), tighten the screws in the bottom hinge. If the door binds at the hinge side (right), the hinge at the bind should be loosened or, if necessary, shimmed out with thin cardboard.

Bind at bottom; tighten bottom hinge.

Chapter 9. If the door binds at the bottom on the latch side, the bottom hinge probably needs tightening. If the door binds on the hinge side, the hinges may be too tight, or may be mortised too deeply into the wood. In this case, remove the affected hinge or hinges and add a shim of thin cardboard under each one; then replace the hinges.

If hinge adjustment doesn't work, you'll have to remove some wood at the binding points. Be very careful in removing any wood; use sandpaper rather than a plane. To prevent future swelling, seal the raw edge with shellac when the weather—and the wood—is dry.

Replacing Door Panels. Many cabinets have flat door panels, either veneered or covered with cloth, cane, metal, or glass. Split panels should be replaced; if the covering of one panel is damaged, all panels should be recovered, if necessary, to match.

Door and drawer panels are usually held in place by molding strips nailed around the edges, sometimes surface-mounted and sometimes set into a rabbet-type joint. These molding strips may be hard to see, but by carefully prying around the panel, you'll be able to see how they're attached.

To replace or recover a panel, remove the molding, using a butt chisel, a knife blade, or the tip of a screwdriver. Be careful not to damage either the molding or the wood. After removing the molding on all four sides, lift the damaged panel out of the frame. Some raised door panels are fastened with screws from the back of the door frame; these screws must be removed before the panel can be taken out. Raised panel doors may be in one piece; in this case, the panel cannot be removed. To repair this type of door, remove the door from its hinges.

On very old furniture, door panels often require special repair techniques. If the panels are held by moldings, remove the moldings very carefully. Try not to bend or damage the nails that hold the moldings; it's best to reuse these nails when you replace the moldings. If the panel is held in the frame in grooves (dadoes), the best way to remove it is to soften the adhesive around the panel with heat or moisture—a hot towel is a good tool. Most old furniture was put together with animal or fish glue, and this adhesive can usually be readily softened. If this doesn't work, take the piece to a professional; the door will have to be taken completely apart, or even cut apart and reassembled.

Panels set in square or rectangular frames are seldom really square. To cut a replacement for any panel, use the old panel as a pattern. Don't try to force a replacement panel in or you may break the frame; if necessary, cut the panel down to fit the frame.

Drawers

Loose Joints. Drawer frame construction is similar to chair construction, with dovetail joints in old or expensive furniture or butt joints, glued and held with corrugated nails, in newer furniture. Dovetail joints seldom separate; if they do, force adhesive into the loose joint and tap the joint together with a hammer. Butt joints are another problem. To tighten a loose butt joint, try gluing the joint and tapping it together as tightly as you can; clamp it firmly until the glue is dry. If this doesn't work,

you may be able to nail the joint through the face of the drawer; countersink the nail heads and fill the holes with wood filler.

Binding. Problems with drawer frames are usually the cause of sticking and binding drawers. When a drawer sticks, it's jerked to get it open and slammed closed; this causes the joints in the frame to separate. First, make sure the joints are tight. Then lubricate the drawer guides and the top and bottom edges of the sides with stick lubricant, wax from a candle, paraffin, or silicone spray. Do not use a petroleum lubricant; oil will collect dirt and dust, and cause more problems than the binding.

If lubrication doesn't solve the problem, carefully sand down the binding points. Remove only as much wood as necessary, and seal the raw wood with shellac to prevent future swelling. If sanding doesn't eliminate binding, examine the drawer's runners and guides.

Worn Guides and Runners. Drawers are built with wood or metal runners, and move back and forth on guides or tracks. In old furniture, the runners are parallel pieces of wood fastened to the drawer bottom, and the guides are strips of wood across the frame. Sometimes the runners or guides are missing; sometimes they're split, warped, or badly worn. Rough guides or runners can cause the drawer to bind, and can eventually damage the frame.

If the drawer guide is missing, install metal guides, available in several lengths and sold in hardware stores and home centers. Complete installation instructions are provided with the guides. If a wood drawer guide is rough, smooth it carefully with sandpaper or a rasp, or—as a last resort—a block plane. If the drawer still binds, remove the guide completely. Break a hacksaw blade in half and wrap one end of it with electricians' tape; wearing gloves, cut the guide out with short strokes of the saw blade.

After removing the old guide, you may be able to install metal guides, as above. For a neater job, cut and fit a new wooden guide, the same size as the old one. Use hardwood to make the guide; softwood wears too quickly. Glue the new guide into position and secure it with nails; countersink the nail heads so they won't interfere with the drawer's operation.

When the runners are worn, the drawer moves unevenly because the wood is uneven. To replace a worn runner, plane and rabbet the worn edge to form an even, smoothly mortised strip along the drawer edge. Glue a thin strip of hardwood into each mortised runner edge, building it up to its original height. Secure the runners with small nails, and countersink the nails so that they won't interfere with the drawer's operation.

If the drawer frame has a wood kicker above the sides, and the kicker is worn, smooth it and add a new hardwood strip to build it up again. Follow the same procedure used to replace worn runners.

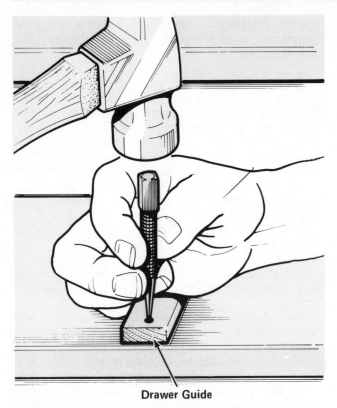

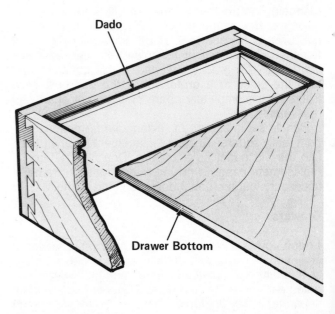

Split Fronts. Split drawer fronts are usually the result of missing drawer guides. First, install drawer guides. Second, repair the split with glue forced into the break. Wipe away any excess glue and lightly clamp the edges with a strap clamp. Use only light pressure; too much pressure will buckle the wood at the split.

Split Bottoms. Drawer bottoms are not fastened into the drawer sides and ends; the bottom panel fits loosely into dadoes in the sides. This permits expansion and contraction of the wood, and prevents the joints from cracking. To replace a drawer bottom, just remove one end of the drawer and slide the bottom panel out. Replace it with a new plywood or hardboard panel cut to fit. Some drawer bottoms are lightly tacked to a piece of molding nailed to the inside edges of the sides and back, and some drawer bottoms are set on triangular glue blocks. Remove these fasteners or braces before disassembling the drawer. If the piece of furniture is an antique, the drawers were probably hand-fashioned. These drawers should *not* be repaired with plywood or hardboard.

Warped Boards

Table leaves and other flat parts can warp unless they're properly sealed, and years of uneven humidity can leave them severely cupped. In most cases, unwarping them isn't too difficult.

Drawer Guide

Replace a wood drawer guide with a new hardwood guide, cut to the same size. Glue and nail the guide into place; countersink the nail heads to prevent binding.

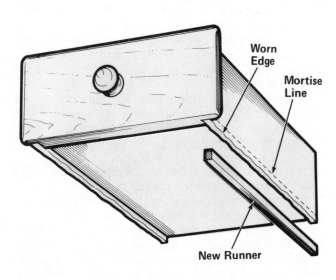

Worn Edge

Mortise Line

New Runner

Plane and rabbet worn runners to form an even mortise along the drawer edge; glue and nail a new hardwood runner into the mortised edge. Countersink the nails.

Dado

Drawer Bottom

The drawer bottom is held by a dado around the sides. To replace a split bottom, remove one end of the drawer; slide the old bottom out and the new one in.

To unwarp a board, work in summer; the traditional cure is exposure to wet grass and hot sun. Water a grassy area thoroughly and set the board curved side up on the wet grass. As the dry side of the board absorbs moisture from the grass, the moist side—the convex side—is dried out by the sun, and the board unwarps. Unless the warp is caused by stress in the wood, the board should straighten out within a day.

When the board has straightened out, clamp it between two straight boards so that it will dry evenly. Before replacing it in the piece of furniture, seal the unfinished side with shellac to prevent it from warping again.

Caning

In antique furniture, caning is usually handwoven; it is threaded through individual holes in the frame, and woven in strand by strand. This type of caning should be replaced by a professional. In most newer furniture, the cane is prewoven; an entire sheet of cane is attached in a groove around the open frame. Sheet cane is easy to replace.

First, remove the old cane. If you can, pull the cane out of the groove, using a chisel to pry up the spline that holds it. If the spline is stubborn, you may have to soak the area with a towel soaked in very hot water and wrung almost dry. When the adhesive has softened, place a block of wood under the caning and tap the block with a hammer. This should dislodge the caning and the spline from the seat frame. After removing the cane, clean out the groove with a chisel. Make sure it's completely clean and dry before you install the new cane.

To replace the cane, buy a new spline and new prewoven sheet caning, about 1 to 1½ inches larger all around than the opening. Make sure the spline is the right width for the groove. Soak the cane and the spline in warm water for about 10 to 15 minutes to soften the fiber.

When the spline and the cane are pliable, blot them dry with a towel. Lay the caning over the groove, shiny side up. Starting at the center of one short side, pound the edge of the caning into the groove with a narrow wood wedge—cut the wedge from a 1 × 2 or a 1 × 3, and use a hammer to tap it along the caning. The bottom of the taper on the wedge should be slightly smaller than the groove. Work along the side of the frame toward the corners, wedging the cane firmly and squarely down into the groove; if it isn't securely wedged, it will come loose.

When the first side of the cane is in place, clamp the caned edge between two pieces of 1 × 2 or 1 × 3 to prevent the caning from popping out of the groove. Then stretch the sheet of cane across the frame and wedge the opposite side, starting at the center and working out. Repeat the procedure, clamping each side as you go, to secure the remaining sides. As you work,

the caning may start to dry out; if necessary, rewet it to keep it pliable.

When the caning has been tapped into the groove all around the frame, trim off any excess at the outside corner of the groove; set a sharp chisel into the groove to cut the cane. Then lay a narrow bead of white glue all around the groove on top of the caning. Blot the spline dry and force it into the groove over the caning, using a wooden or rubber mallet to drive it into the groove. Pull the spline tight as you go, and ease it around the corners. You may have to install the spline in several pieces; if so, make sure the ends butt together tightly to form a continuous spline. Finally, wipe off any excess glue.

Let the glue and the cane dry completely; as it dries, the caning will become taut. Let the job set for at least a week before you use it.

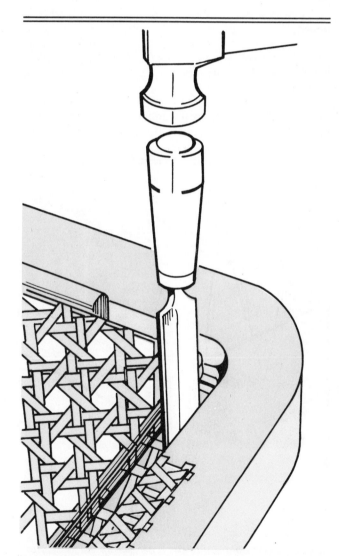

When the caning is firmly wedged into the groove all around the opening, trim off the excess cane with a sharp chisel, set straight into the outside corner of the groove.

Mirror and Picture Frames

Although frames are really not pieces of furniture, they do play a role in furnishing, and some frames can be very valuable. Antique frames were usually made from solid cabinet wood, such as walnut, cherry, or mahogany—wood that's both hard to find and expensive today. For this reason, most old frames are well worth repairing.

Loose Joints. The usual problem with frames is separating miter joints. There are several ways to fix open miter joints, but the easiest way is glue. Force glue into the open joint with a glue injector and clamp it with a corner or a strap clamp. Look for metal fasteners along the edges of the joint; if necessary, drive them back into the wood after the clamp closes the gap in the joint.

If the joint won't stay closed, it can be glued and nailed; drill pilot holes to prevent the wood from splitting. You can either leave the nails flush with the surface of the wood or countersink them and fill the holes. If you leave the nails exposed, use decorative nails such as brass.

If the frame is a valuable antique, and you don't want to use nails, close the joint with a corner spline. Clamp the frame in a vise, padding the wood with a piece of carpet or a thick layer of cloth. With a ripsaw, cut a notch into and across the corners of the joint along the edge of the frame, as illustrated. Cut a thin piece of matching wood to fit into the saw cut; test it in the cut and adjust it as necessary. Spread a thin coating of glue onto both sides of the spline, insert the spline into the cut, and pull the joint together with a strap clamp. Let the glue dry completely. Then, with a sharp block plane, trim the edges of the spline flush with the surface of the frame, and sand them smooth. Spot-finish the spline area to match, or refinish the entire frame.

Damaged Carvings. Chipped frames can be patched with a thick mixture of spackling compound or plaster of paris. Roughly form the design you want to duplicate with the patching compound. Position the rough patch material and lightly press it against the frame; then, with the tip of a craft knife or a toothpick, final-shape the compound so it blends in with the design. It will probably be impossible to match the design exactly, but the repair won't be noticeable.

Let the patch dry completely, and then spot-stain or paint it to blend it with the rest of the frame. Test the colors on a chunk of dried spackling compound or plaster of paris before you apply the mixture to the frame repair. You should be able to color-blend the patch perfectly.

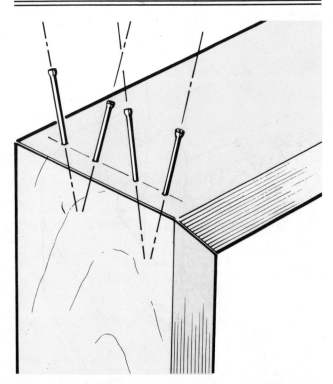

If glue doesn't hold a mitered corner, secure the joint with nails, driven into the wood at a slight angle. Drill pilot holes to keep the wood from splitting; leave the nail heads flush or countersink them.

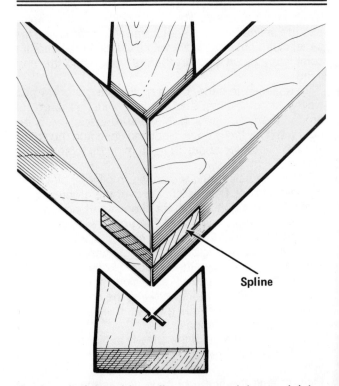

Spline

To close the joint with a spline, cut a notch into each joint edge; cut a thin spline from matching wood. Glue the spline into place and clamp the joint closed; when the glue is dry, trim the spline flush with the frame.